A Guide to Better Spelling

Second Edition

Angela Burt

Stanley Thornes (Publishers) Ltd.

Cartoons by Tim Archbold

First published in 1985 (ISBN 0–85950–343–7) by:
Stanley Thornes (Publishers) Ltd
Ellenborough House
Wellington Street
CHELTENHAM GL50 1YW
England

Second Edition 1991

99   00   /   10   9   8

British Library Cataloguing in Publication Data
Burt, A.M. (Angela M.)
   A guide to better spelling.—2nd ed.
   I. Title
   428.1

ISBN 0–7487–1234–8

Typeset by Tech-Set, Gateshead, Tyne & Wear.
Printed and bound in Great Britain by
Redwood Books, Trowbridge, Wiltshire

CONTENTS

PREFACE   vi

ACKNOWLEDGEMENTS   viii

CHAPTER ONE   **Forming plurals**

Regular plurals (Rule 1)   1

Nouns ending in sibilants (Rule 2)   2

Nouns ending in –y (Rule 3)   6

Nouns ending in –o (Rule 4)   12

Nouns ending in –f and –fe (Rule 5)   16

Other plurals   24

     Mutated plurals   24

     Nouns with the same singular
     and plural form   24

     Nouns which have no
     singular form   25

     Plurals of compound words   25

     Foreign nouns with two
     plurals   26

     Foreign nouns which retain
     foreign plurals   27

CHAPTER TWO   **Adding suffixes**

One-one-one words (Rule 6)   28

Magic–e words (Rule 7)   33

Revision exercises based on
Rules 6 and 7   39

The –Y rule expanded (Rule 8)   42

Two-one-one words (Rule 9)   48

–able/ible   61

–ant, –ance/–ent, –ence   62

–cal/–cle   63

–ceed, –cede, –sede   64

–ful   65

CHAPTER THREE **Adding prefixes**
Common prefixes 67
The five chameleons 70

CHAPTER FOUR **Words often confused**
accept/except 75
affect/effect 75
all most/almost 75
allowed/aloud 75
all ready/already 75
all right 76
all so/also 76
all together/altogether 76
all ways/always 76
a lot 76
any way/anyway 76
boarder/border 76
breath/breathe 76
cannot 76
clothes/cloths 77
complement/compliment 77
councillor/counsellor 77
dairy/diary 77
desert/dessert 77
heroin/heroine 77
in fact 77
in front 78
its/it's 78
knew/new 78
know/no 78
licence/license 78
lightening/lightning 78
loose/lose 78
of/off 79
past/passed 79
personal/personnel 79
practice/practise 79
principal/principle 80

	quiet/quite	80
	seam/seem	80
	shore/sure	80
	some times/sometimes	80
	stationary/stationery	80
	thank you/thank-you	80
	their/there/they're	80
	to/too/two	81
	upstairs	81
	weather/whether	81
	were/where	81
	who's/whose	81
	your/you're	82
	Exercises on words often confused	82
CHAPTER FIVE	**Useful tips**	
	Ie/ei words	96
	Extra k	100
	Words often mispronounced	102
	Learning strategies	104
	Use your eyes	104
	Use your ears	107
	Use your writing hand	108
	Proof-reading	109
ANSWERS TO EXERCISES		111

PREFACE

Some people seem to be naturally 'good spellers'; many others find spelling miserably confusing and feel themselves doomed to failure again and again. 'I'm rubbish at spelling' and 'I can't spell' and 'I've never been able to spell' are depressingly familiar self-judgements.

Such students need a helping hand if they are to see patterns, for example, in the modifications necessary when adding some suffixes. They need help if they are to learn to utilise their knowledge of one word to help them to spell another. They need to be shown ways of distinguishing between homophones. They need to be shown strategies for learning notoriously tricky words that have to be tackled individually. They need to acquire confidence. Indeed, they need to begin to relish some of the very idiosyncrasies of English spelling that depressed them before, and when they begin to work at words with pleasure the battle is won.

I have felt passionate about the teaching of spelling for many years now and I am a strong advocate of the value of a structured approach to the teaching of spelling not only for dyslexic students but for all hesitant spellers. I teach spelling that way and I know it works.

When preparing this second edition of *A Guide to Better Spelling* (the book was first published in 1982), I was much heartened by reading in the Cox Report ('English 5–16', June 1989):

> With regard to spelling, the aim should be that by the end of compulsory schooling, pupils should be able to spell confidently most of the words that they are likely to need to use frequently in their writing; to recognise those aspects of English spelling that are systematic; to make a sensible attempt to spell words that they have not seen before; to check their work for misspellings and to use a dictionary.

I hope that this book helps in some measure to realise these aims. It has been written with just such a purpose in mind.

I have written the book particularly for students at Key Stages 2, 3 and 4 and for older students who may be studying on their own. Answers are provided at the back of the book where appropriate. In practice this also makes the book very useful when a teacher wants to direct pupils' attention to patterns that they are regularly getting wrong. Pupils can read the guidelines, work through an exercise and check that the spelling pattern or generalisation has been understood. The book then is useful for either class or private study.

I am grateful to Tim Archbold for his lively cartoons and I hope this book is fun to use as well as a really helpful guide.

Angela Burt
Exmouth 1991

ACKNOWLEDGEMENTS

The publisher wishes to acknowledge the following for their kind permission to reproduce material:

The Times	*Festina Lente* (pages 21–2, adapted)
The Sunday Times	*Friction across the Fence* (pages 58–9, abridged)
Express & Echo	*Virging on the Ridiculous* (page 106)

Chapter One

FORMING PLURALS

In this chapter, we deal with five very useful rules which govern the formation of most plurals in English. Most plurals are perfectly regular and so these five rules or patterns are well worth knowing.

At the very end of the chapter, for reference, are some less common plurals.

Regular plurals and nouns ending in sibilants

Rule 1

The plural of most nouns is formed by adding **s** to the singular.

doors	tables	bicycles
ceilings	chairs	books
flags	windows	gardens

Rule 2

Nouns which end in a **sibilant** (a hissing sound) need **es** to be added in the plural, unless they already end in –e.

(Say the plurals below aloud. You will then *hear* that a syllable is being added. This should help you when you need to spell the form.)

class**es**	tax**es**	waltz**es**	arch**es**	flush**es**
atlas**es**	hoax**es**	fez**es**	porch**es**	wish**es**
bus**es**	box**es**		bench**es**	squash**es**

Add **s**

stitch**es**	size**s**
latch**es**	house**s**
hutch**es**	rose**s**

EXERCISE 1

Form the plural of these words by adding **s** or **es** as required.

1) Sophie was in tears because eight of her hen___ had been killed by fox___.

2) The two rabbit hutch___ are in a dreadful state.

3) Mr Ponsford collects clock___ and has a marvellous collection.

4) Mini-bus driver__ are usually very helpful.

5) The fifth-years are carrying out a survey of the church__ and chapel__ in the area.

6) Will you pack away the bench__?

7) All the house__ need re-roofing.

8) Both box__ of firework__ were damp.

9) Don't believe a word he says. His hunch__ are never reliable.

10) The witch__ in *Macbeth,* or the three weird sister__ as they are called, are usually depicted as two aged crone__ and a younger woman.

When you have checked your work against the answers at the back of the book, look again at any mistakes you have made. Remember that you can always hear the extra syllable –es at the end of a word. If you are in doubt as to whether you need **s** or **es**, **say the plural word to yourself and listen carefully**.

EXERCISE 2

–s or –es? (Listen carefully and aim to get every plural right this time.)

1) Someone had scribbled over all the notice__ and the Principal was furious.

2) Bus___ and coach___ will no longer be allowed to stop outside the school.

3) Both cat___ are asleep in the most comfortable chair___.

4) Lunch___ have improved in the refectory since staff bonus___ have been introduced.

5) What an unsavoury collection of tee-shirt___, sock___ and jeans!

6) He's a bully who made Fiona thoroughly miserable with all kinds of pinch___, punch___, kick___ and nudg___. He deserves a taste of his own medicine.

7) Alternating shower___ and sunny spell___ are forecast for tomorrow.

8) Member___ of the jury, this woman is innocent.

9) I lost three inch___ round my waist after a week on the banana diet.

10) Actress___, actor___, and producer___ will all be affected by the new Equity ruling.

EXERCISE 3

Prepared Dictation (Testing Rules 1 and 2)

Read through the following passage very carefully. The fifteen plurals governed by Rules 1 and 2 have been underlined. Make sure that you can spell these. Ten troublesome words that are frequently misspelt are listed too. Learn these by heart and any other words you are unsure of. When you have prepared the dictation thoroughly, ask someone to dictate the passage to you.

It was extremely dark and he felt tired, frightened and lonely as he tried to make his way through the <u>trees</u>, <u>brambles</u> and <u>ferns</u> of the forest. <u>Owls</u> watched him from high <u>branches</u> and <u>foxes</u> from the cover of <u>bushes</u>. It would be another forty <u>minutes</u> at least before he glimpsed the <u>lights</u> of the <u>cottages</u> on the forest <u>edges</u>. His thin clothes offered little protection against the icy <u>fingers</u> of the wind and the <u>tugs</u> and <u>snatches</u> of the <u>thorns</u>.

These words in the passage may cause trouble. Notice particularly the parts of the word in bold type.

1) extr**eme**ly

2) ti**re**d

3) frighten**ed**

4) lon**e**ly

5) tri**e**d

6) forest

7) an**oth**er

8) f**or**ty

9) min**ute**s

10) cloth**es**

5

Spelling Notebook

A small alphabetically indexed notebook (like an address book) makes an ideal personal spelling dictionary. It would be a very good idea if you were to note down the correct version of every word you misspell as you work your way through this book. Make sure you include all the words you frequently need and over which you hesitate. In this way you will quickly isolate the words that cause you particular difficulty (and identifying them is actually half the battle!). You'll know where to find them quickly when you need them, and you will be helping yourself to learn the correct versions every time you look them up.

Nouns ending in -y

Next comes a most useful rule. It looks a little complicated at first but it is well worth studying carefully. Errors in forming the plural of words ending in –y are very common in students' work but there is really no excuse. This is a rule which has only one very minor exception, as you will see.

In pairs, see if you can work out the spelling pattern for yourself.

Singular	Plural
boy	boys
alley	alleys
day	days
buoy	buoys
key	keys
guy	guys
ray	rays
turkey	turkeys

Singular	Plural
hob**by**	hobb**ies**
centu**ry**	centur**ies**
bo**dy**	bod**ies**
ba**by**	bab**ies**
la**dy**	lad**ies**
quali**ty**	qualit**ies**
ci**ty**	cit**ies**
par**ty**	part**ies**

Rule 3

If there's a vowel (a, e, i, o, u) before the final **y**, just add **s** to form the plural.

chimn**ey**   chimn**eys**

If there's a consonant before the **y**, change the **y** to **i** and add **es**.

opportuni**ty**   opportuni**ties**

EXERCISE 4

You can be so confident about this rule not letting you down, that you can apply it to these nonsense words and form the plurals correctly. Try the following words and see.

1) peloy

2) aromy

3) garulomophity

4) sizergey

5) bethray   8) drahiy

6) zuy   9) carulasophy

7) krosky   10) eszphyxinimity

● Use **boy/boys** as a memory key so that you can deduce
  how all words ending in <u>a vowel and y</u> will form their
  plurals. You then know it's the other lot that ends in **–ies**.

EXERCISE 5

Spelling Quiz on –Y Words

Rules (It's always best to agree competition rules before
hand. These work well.)

1) Divide the class into two, three or four teams
   according to numbers and seating arrangements.

2) The teacher acts as quizmaster <u>and</u> scorer.

3) The teacher/quizmaster chooses questions at
   random from the list on pages 9–10 so that no-one
   knows what's coming next.

4) <u>Team members do not volunteer to answer the</u>
   <u>question when they've heard it!</u> The quizmaster
   chooses who is going to answer the question and
   then asks the question. (The aim is that everyone
   should have answered a question by the end of the
   quiz.)

5) Pupils selected to answer questions have to decide
   immediately on hearing the question whether to
   risk answering it unaided for two marks or to play
   safe and confer with the rest of the team for one

mark. Whatever they decide, the pupil originally selected to answer the question must remain as the spokesperson.

6) If the question is wrongly answered and the correct answer is not by then too obvious, (it will be on this occasion!), it may be appropriate to offer it for a bonus of one mark to the first volunteer from the other team(s) to raise a hand. It can be subsequently offered again and this time volunteers from the original team can offer to answer.

7) The quizmaster's decisions are always final and s(he) will ensure that no-one takes the quiz too seriously but that everyone learns some spellings.

1 pony	14 jelly
2 ally	15 jersey
3 attorney	16 factory
4 alloy	17 puppy
5 library	18 laboratory
6 turkey	19 pasty
7 lady	20 jockey
8 baby	21 city
9 activity	22 navy
10 enemy	23 quality
11 donkey	24 fantasy
12 lorry	25 battery
13 abbey	26 society

27 eccentricity	34 butterfly
28 ecstasy	35 quantity
29 quay	36 key
30 gipsy	37 opportunity
31 kidney	38 travesty
32 story	39 galaxy
33 trolley	40 duty

The only exception to the –Y rule is this: the plurals of **proper nouns** (i.e. names of places, people etc.) ending in <u>consonant + y</u> are formed simply by adding **s**. This keeps the name intact and therefore recognisable.

> There were three **MARYS** in the class. (Mary Gillespie, Mary Hunt and Mary Rowden)
> There were two **MARIES**. (Marie Clancy and Marie Greenham)
> We saw the **HARDYS** last night. (i.e. Mr and Mrs Hardy)
> We invited the **HARDIES** to supper. (i.e. Mr and Mrs Hardie)

EXERCISE 6

Prepared Dictation (Testing Rule 3: the –Y Rule)

Read the passage very carefully, making sure you understand the underlined words which are governed by Rule 3. Make sure you learn the other words in the cautionary list if you are uncertain of them. Check that there are no other words in the passage that will cause you difficulty. When you are ready, ask for the passage to be dictated.

On a certain Saturday in August, the sun was shining, <u>ponies</u> were exercising in the small ring and <u>babies</u> cried as <u>turkeys</u> gobbled and <u>donkeys</u> brayed. Exhausted <u>families</u> and <u>parties</u> of mischievous children picnicked among the <u>daisies</u>. Always a pleasant occasion, the eighth annual County Show was in progress and would continue for four <u>days</u>, providing <u>opportunities</u> for farmers to view the latest equipment. There were more stands this year and vastly improved <u>facilities</u>.

SPELLING HAZARDS

1) cert**ai**n

2) Sat**ur**day

3) shi**n**ing

4) ex**er**cising

5) cri**e**d

6) ex**h**austed

7) misch**ievous**

8) picnic**k**ed

9) am**ong**

10) al**w**ays

11) ple**a**sant

12) oc**ca**sion

13) eig**hth**

14) an**nn**ual

15) vi**ew**

16) equi**pm**ent

Nouns ending in -o

This is a very interesting group of words. Most nouns ending in –o form their plural by adding **s**. There are very few exceptions but some of these exceptions are frequently used words and cause a lot of trouble as a result.

Rule 4

Most nouns ending in –o form their plural by adding **S**. These include:

● **all musical nouns**	solos, sopranos
● **all nouns of Spanish and Italian origin**	armadillos, casinos
● **all abbreviated nouns**	discos, photos
● **all nouns ending in a double vowel**	studios, igloos

There are **twenty-three exceptions** to Rule 4 which require **es**. (The ten most common words are in bold print.)

buffaloes	**heroes**	**potatoes**
calicoes	**innuendoes**	stuccoes
cargoes	jingoes	**tomatoes**
desperadoes	mangoes	tornadoes
dingoes	**mosquitoes**	torpedoes
dominoes	**Negroes**	vetoes
echoes	noes	**volcanoes**
embargoes	peccadilloes	

POTAT**OES**
TOMAT**OES**
We are exceptions
Please keep us on our TOES

These plurals can be **s** or **es** (you can't go wrong with these!)

archipelagos	*or*	archipelagoes
Eskimos	*or*	Eskimoes
flamingos	*or*	flamingoes
frescos	*or*	frescoes
grottos	*or*	grottoes
halos	*or*	haloes
mementos	*or*	mementoes
mottos	*or*	mottoes
placebos	*or*	placeboes
provisos	*or*	provisoes
stilettos	*or*	stilettoes
zeros	*or*	zeroes

● **Note**   The plural of librett**o** is librett**i**
            virtuos**o** is virtuos**i**

EXERCISE 7

In pairs, look at the fifteen plurals that follow and decide which category in Rule 4 applies to each.

Example   **sopranos**: all musical nouns ending in –o add **s** in the plural.

13

1) zoos	6) cuckoos	11) rodeos
2) lassos	7) banjos	12) scenarios
3) tattoos	8) kangaroos	13) casinos
4) radios	9) shampoos	14) sopranos
5) cellos	10) photos	15) oratorios

EXERCISE 8

Refresh your memory of Rule 4 if you wish before attempting this exercise. Try to complete it without looking at the rule again.

1) We saw (cargo) of (tomato) and (potato) being unloaded.

2) The visit to the television (studio) was really enjoyable.

3) The little girls looked charming in their (kimono).

4) Old Mr Ponsonby has a huge collection of (curio).

5) The mock raid by (commando) was meant to be the highlight of the display.

6) The (manifesto) of all three parties were delivered the day before polling day.

7) He earns a living composing (motto) for Christmas crackers.

8) Keep both coins as (memento) of your visit.

9) He's built three (gazebo) already.

10) (Echo) of her bullying voice died gradually away.

EXERCISE 9

Prepared Dictation (Testing Rule 4)

Read the passage carefully, noting the underlined words which are governed by Rule 4. Learn any of the words in the cautionary list that you feel uncertain about and make sure there are no other 'danger areas' or words you cannot spell.

Here are copies of the <u>photos</u> we took on our Mediterranean holiday. The embarrassing one of us in <u>sombreros</u> outside the restaurant will amuse you. It was a good holiday. The children went to <u>discos</u> in the hotel every night; we were given complimentary tickets for two excellent concerts. The <u>sopranos</u> and <u>contraltos</u> were magnificent. We'll keep the programmes as <u>mementoes</u>. The food was lovely. How olive oil and tarragon transform <u>tomatoes</u>! I had <u>mangoes</u> for the first time. The <u>mosquitoes</u> were annoying when we ate outside but no <u>volcanoes</u> erupted.

SPELLING HAZARDS

1) copies
2) Mediterranean
3) holiday
4) embarrassing
5) restaurant
6) complimentary
7) excellent
8) annoying
9) **ate**
8) erupted

15

Nouns ending in -f and -fe

The rule for these nouns is a beautifully simple one with which to end the chapter and the exceptions are easy because your ear is the guide.

Rule 5

Nouns ending in –f and –fe add **s** to form the plural.

roof**s**	safe**s**
handkerchief**s**	carafe**s**
sheriff**s**	giraffe**s**

There are **thirteen exceptions** to this rule but don't be alarmed. You can always *hear* **–ves**.

wi**ves**	shel**ves**
kni**ves**	shea**ves**
li**ves**	lea**ves**
cal**ves**	loa**ves**
hal**ves**	thie**ves**
el**ves**	wol**ves**
sel**ves**	

There are **four** words which can be spelt either **fs** or **ves**. Use whichever spelling you prefer but be prepared to see both versions in your reading.

hoofs	*or*	hooves
scarfs	*or*	scarves
turfs	*or*	turves
wharfs	*or*	wharves

If in doubt about **f** or **v**, say the word aloud and listen carefully. (You may have to learn to pronounce the words correctly in one or two cases. Not everybody says **roofs** and **handkerchiefs** correctly.)

EXERCISE 10

Form the plural of these words. Look back at Rule 5 whenever you want to.

1) wife
2) carafe
3) cliff
4) half
5) proof

6) dwarf
7) cast-off
8) flagstaff
9) knife
10) chief

EXERCISE 11

Try to do this exercise *without* looking back at the rule. Trust your ear this time.

1) bailiff
2) life

3) thief
4) hoof

5) giraffe	8) tariff
6) café	9) sheriff
7) muff	10) gulf

EXERCISE 12

Treat this exercise as a revision exercise. Read through Rule 5 once again and make sure you understand it completely before attempting the exercise from memory.

Form the plural of the words in brackets.

1) A pack of (wolf) was slinking through the shadows.

2) Meat and other (foodstuff) are now very scarce in Romania.

3) My great-aunt has sent me a box of lace-edged (handkerchief).

4) Polish ships were unloading at the (wharf).

5) The laughing girls were wearing long football (scarf).

6) The deserted cottages had dilapidated (roof).

7) His (shelf) were loaded with mathematic text-books.

8) Some beautiful fish live on coral (reef).

9) The (thief) ransacked the seaside café.

10) The cows stood contentedly beside their (calf).

EXERCISE 13

Prepared Dictation (Testing Rule 5)

The King of the <u>Dwarfs</u> had quarrelled with the Queen of the <u>Elves</u> and there was a definite threat of war. The King and his advisers decided that <u>wives</u> and families should be evacuated immediately and normal business should be suspended. Extraordinary emergency plans were drawn up: <u>roofs</u> of government buildings were strengthened, millions of <u>loaves</u> were baked, and ninety cannon were positioned on <u>cliffs</u> and <u>wharfs</u>. The <u>chiefs</u> <u>themselves</u> recognised that many <u>lives</u> might be lost.

SPELLING HAZARDS

1) qua**rre**lled

2) defin**i**te

3) advis**e**rs

4) fam**ili**es

5) bu**si**ness

6) extr**ao**rdinary

7) emerg**e**ncy

8) gover**n**ment

9) nin**e**ty

10) reco**g**nised

EXERCISE 14

Revision Quiz (All Five Rules)

Form the plural.

1) radio

2) crutch

3) loaf

4) butterfly

5) echo	23) hero
6) envoy	24) understudy
7) tattoo	25) city
8) avocado	26) knife
9) elf	27) princess
10) entry	28) pulley
11) cargo	29) secretary
12) wallaby	30) half
13) kangaroo	31) moustache
14) lorry	32) calf
15) penalty	33) mosquito
16) scratch	34) duty
17) mass	35) leaf
18) yo-yo	36) galaxy
19) potato	37) heiress
20) thief	38) glass
21) pinch	39) lynx
22) chorus	40) torpedo

EXERCISE 15

Pair Work

Test your proof-reading skills!

Twenty deliberate spelling mistakes have been introduced into the article below which were not present when it originally appeared in *The Times*. Ten plurals have been misspelt and ten other everyday words which students often find difficult.

FESTINA LENTE

A week after the fastest motorist ever to appear befor a British court made history in County Durham, one of the slowest was penalized by magistrates in South Wales. The former, who was fined £800 after outpacing the police of three countys in his Porsche, deserves scant public sympathy. The latter, in more waies than one, should give pause for thought.

Mr Myrddin Thomas, aged 53, a one-time miner, was fined by the Bench at Pontypridd for driveing at only 20 miles an hour. A policeman, who in this case had little trouble catching up with him, booked him for holding up a two-mile queue of traffic.

The charge was that he piloted his Marina without resonable consideration for other road users. He paid £15 costs in addition to his fine, had his license endorsed and was handed two penalty pointes.

This sounds unjust. The offence for which he was brought before the court is one which covers a multitude of irritants. Had he deliberately obstructed other motorists or driven in an agressive manner, one might well find oneself in agrement with the Bench. But there would seem to have been no sujestion of that.

Most drivers know the fealings of frustration which come from being caught behind slow-moving vehicles on roads which allow little scope for overtaking. A tractor pulling a wagonload of hay or a familly car with a caravan in tow can provoke long ques and frayed tempers. The Highway Code lectures drivers of such vechicles on the need to pull into the side whenever possible. That is sound advice which all motorists should heed.

But Mr Thomas was driving at 20 mph in a 30 mph limit zone. This might have been slower than road conditions warranted. But life is full of minor irritations which people must endure every day. Mr Thomas was surley within his rights to do so. What's more, he was driving very safely. For the chairman of the magistrates to say that he might have caused other motorists to crash is surely a very questionable statement.

The assumption must be that the drivers stuck behind him might loose there patience and take unwonted risks to overtake him. But could Mr Thomas himself be blamed for that?

A former lorry driver on a radio phone-in two nights ago related how he was fined £10 meny years ago (when £10 was a draconian penalty) for also driving at 23 miles an hour. But in his case he was charged with going too fast. 'We'll keep you speed merchants off the road,' declared the magistrate.

It is still the 'speed merchants' whom we need to prosecute, like the 150 mph Herr Randolf Off who completed a 45-mile journey in 16 minutes. If everyone drove around like Mr Thomas, the pace of life would undoubtedly slow down. But the roads would surely be safer – not more dangerous.

Had the policeman who apprehended the ex-miner advised him to pull in for several minutes to allow the motorists behind him to pass by, a sensable compromise might be said to have been reached. As it is the prosecution of Mr Thomas was not only of dubious legal merit but has sent the wrong signal to motorists in Britain.

We need to encourage patient sober driving, not the manic machismo that often now prevails. Mr Thomas might have carried this policy rather far. But to arraign him for doing so is to drive a horse and cart through Whitehall policys – an image which in this case seems rather apposite.

The Times, 26 August 1989
© Times Newspapers Ltd 1989

Use dictionaries, spelling notebooks, this book and any reference book that can help, if you wish. When you have finished, check your findings with the answers at the back.

EXERCISE 16

This is a revision test on all the words in the cautionary lists accompanying the prepared dictation exercises in this chapter. Ask someone to dictate them to you.

1) ate
2) tried
3) cried
4) picnicked
5) erupted
6) quarrelled
7) recognised
8) tired
9) frightened
10) exhausted
11) shining
12) embarrassing
13) exercising
14) annoying
15) extremely
16) always
17) forest
18) minutes
19) clothes
20) Saturday
21) occasion
22) view
23) equipment
24) copies
25) Mediterranean
26) holiday
27) restaurant
28) advisers
29) families
30) business
31) emergency
32) government
33) lonely
34) eighth
35) forty
36) ninety
37) certain
38) mischievous
39) pleasant
40) another
41) annual
42) extraordinary
43) excellent
44) definite
45) complimentary
46) among

Other plurals

Before we leave plurals altogether, let us look at some plurals which do not come within the scope of our five rules. You will see that some words change internally (mutated plurals), some have the same form whether they are singular or plural, and some have no singular form at all. I have also listed some compound words because these need care in the plural. For reference also I have listed some foreign words in fairly frequent use with their plurals. Sometimes you have a choice between an English and a foreign plural; sometimes only the foreign plural is available. Remember that all these irregular plurals are given in a good dictionary.

Mutated plurals

child	→	children
die	→	dice
foot	→	feet
goose	→	geese
louse	→	lice
man	→	men
mouse	→	mice
ox	→	oxen
penny	→	pence
tooth	→	teeth
woman	→	women

Nouns with the same singular and plural form

aircraft	deer	salmon
cannon	forceps	swine
cod	grouse (bird)	trout

Nouns which have no singular form

alms	riches
bellows	scissors
binoculars	secateurs
breeches	shears
eaves	spectacles
gallows	thanks
measles	tidings
news	tongs
pants	trousers
pincers	tweezers
pliers	victuals

and all –ics words, e.g. athletics
mathematics
politics etc.

Plurals of compound words

- If the noun comes last in a compound word, make it plural in the usual way.

blackberry	blackberries
by-stander	by-standers
wash-basin	wash-basins
wrist-watch	wrist-watches

- If the noun comes first in a compound word, still make that noun plural.

court-martial	courts-martial
son-in-law	sons-in-law
passer-by	passers-by
maid-of-honour	maids-of-honour
knight-errant	knights-errant
hanger-on	hangers-on

- If the noun has the suffix –ful, add **S**

spoonful	spoonfuls
cupful	cupfuls

- Sometimes when two nouns form a compound word, both nouns are made plural.

manservant	menservants
Lord Justice	Lords Justices
Trade Union	Trades Unions

Foreign nouns

Some foreign nouns have both English and foreign plurals

appendix	→	appendices
		appendixes
automaton	→	automata
		automatons
bureau	→	bureaux
		bureaus
formula	→	formulae
		formulas
fungus	→	fungi
		funguses
hiatus	→	hiatus
		hiatuses
hippopotamus	→	hippopotami
		hippotamuses
index	→	indices
		indexes
memorandum	→	memoranda
		memorandums
nucleus	→	nuclei
		nucleuses
portmanteau	→	portmanteaux
		portmanteaus
plateau	→	plateaux
		plateaus

Other foreign words retain their foreign endings

This is not an exhaustive list.

addendum	→	addenda
analysis	→	analyses
antenna	→	antennae
axis	→	axes
basis	→	bases
criterion	→	criteria
crisis	→	crises
datum	→	data
erratum	→	errata
hypothesis	→	hypotheses
libretto	→	libretti
nebula	→	nebulae
oasis	→	oases
parenthesis	→	parentheses
phenomenon	→	phenomena
radius	→	radii
stimulus	→	stimuli
stratum	→	strata
synopsis	→	synopses
tableau	→	tableaux
terminus	→	termini
thesis	→	theses
tumulus	→	tumuli

Chapter Two

ADDING SUFFIXES

In this chapter, we deal with **suffixes**. A suffix is a syllable (or syllables) added at the **end** of a word. With most words in English, we tack on a suffix and that is that. However, there are circumstances where we have to exercise great care.

Have you ever been guilty of writing 'The sun was <u>shinning</u> brightly' or 'I did not find her <u>arguement</u> convincing'? Have you ever sent a horse '<u>gallopping</u> over the moor' or claimed that your heroine 'walked <u>saddly</u> away'? It is errors such as these that we are concerned with here.

There are four spelling rules or patterns which govern the spelling modifications needed when you add endings to some words. Let's take a closer look at them.

One-one-one words

Look at these words and find three things that they all have in common.

spot	fit	beg	pad
mud	plan	mop	hot
net	throb	sad	thin

Each word is **one** syllable, ending in **one** consonant preceded by **one** vowel.

A convenient way of referring to such words is to call them **one-one-one** words.

What happens when you add suffixes to one-one-one words?

Rule 6

There is no change to one-one-one words when adding a **consonant** suffix.

hot	**hot**ly	fit	**fit**ness
spot	**spot**less	sin	**sin**ful

You double the final consonant of one-one-one words when you add a **vowel** suffix.

hot	**hott**er	fit	**fitt**est
spot	**spott**ed	sin	**sinn**ing

● This rule does *not* apply to words like **cOOl** (two vowels) and **daRN** (two consonants at end). These words are quite straightforward, and suffixes can be added without any modification (**COOL**ing winds; she was **DARN**ing socks). One-one-one words, on the other hand, sometimes double their final consonant (**SPOTT**ed) and sometimes do not (**SPOT**less) as we have seen. Remember these two words or any other pair you happen to know already as a memory key to the one-one-one spelling rule.

● **Y** is sometimes a vowel and sometimes a consonant.

It is a **vowel** at the **end** of words and syllables.

boy   **muddy** (mud + **y**)

It is a **consonant** at the **beginning** of words and syllables.

yolk   **beyond** (be + **yond**)

EXERCISE 17

Add these consonant suffixes to base words after checking the rule to see whether any modification to the spelling of the base word will be necessary.

1) prim + ly
2) fret + ful
3) rim + less
4) thin + ly
5) sad + ness

EXERCISE 18

Add these vowel suffixes to base words after checking the rule to see whether any modification to the spelling of the base word will be necessary.

1) lop + ed
2) beg + ar
3) scan + ing
4) sun + y
5) run + er

EXERCISE 19

All the words in brackets are one-one-one words, as you can see. Join the base words and suffixes, doubling the final consonant of the base word where necessary.

1) The Queen was cheered loudly as she (step + ed) out of her new Mini.

2) Don't stand there (chat + ing) when there is work to be done.

3) We (pat + ed) the spaniel dry.

4) The light breeze barely (stir + ed) the leaves.

5) Sarah read her bank statement (glum + ly).

6) Why are your shoes so (mud + y)?

7) There's always one (rot + en) peach in a pack of ten.

8) There were (drop + lets) of rain caught in the spiders' webs.

9) She's a (fit + ness) freak. She runs miles every day.

10) Matt can be surprisingly (wit + y) when he's in the right mood.

EXERCISE 20

Two-minute brainteaser

This exercise, which requires all the suffixes in the right-hand column to be joined to appropriate base words in the left-hand column, is more difficult than it looks. **You can use each suffix once only**. Beware of 'wasting' it on a base word that is capable of various combinations when you may need to reserve it for a base word that can take that suffix and no other. Make sure you double the final consonant when you add a vowel suffix:

Base words	Suffixes
1) sad	–ful
2) thin	–est
3) bad	–ed
4) hug	–less
5) sin	–ing
6) dip	–ness
7) win	–er
8) fun	–some
9) big	–y
10) sun	–ly

- **Note** Remember that one-syllabled words like **quit** come within the scope of our rule. We shall have to consider the obligatory **u** after the **q** as part of that consonant, followed by one vowel and one consonant. Thus we have **quitted**, **quitting**.

- There are a few exceptions to the one-one-one rule but I don't think they will cause you any difficulty. The exceptions are easily summarised. **Never double the final consonant if the word ends in W, X, or Y.** So we have **paw**ing, **wax**ed, **lay**ing. (These words would look very peculiar with double letters!) You can apply the rule safely in every other case provided the word is one-one-one.

32

EXERCISE 21

Prepared Dictation (Testing Rule 6)

My neighbour decided to make her niece a woollen skirt as a surprise present and I volunteered to help. <u>Fitting</u> the pattern pieces on to the material was quite awkward but we finally <u>pinned</u> everything in place and started <u>cutting</u> out. Once that was done, we stitched <u>madly</u> away. It was pleasant <u>sitting</u> opposite each other in that familiar <u>sunny</u> room and <u>chatting</u>. The skirt was soon <u>hemmed</u>, <u>pressed</u> and <u>slipped</u> on to a hanger. We had finished and we <u>grinned</u> happily.

SPELLING HAZARDS

1) n**ei**ghbour
2) de**ci**ded
3) n**ie**ce
4) w**oo**llen
5) s**ur**prise

6) vol**unt**eered
7) **aw**kward
8) ple**asa**nt
9) famil**ia**r
10) fini**shed**

Magic -e words

Look carefully at these examples.

a) She **planned** her work carefully. (to **plan**)
b) He **tapped** nervously on the door. (to **tap**)
c) The rabbit **hopped** across the lawn. (to **hop**)

The verbs in bold print above are all one-one-one words, coming within the scope of the rule we have just studied.

Such words are often confused with words ending in a **magic –e** (sometimes called **silent –e**, **mute –e**, or even **lazy –e**). Examples of magic –e words are given in the four sentences below.

d) He **planed** the wood lovingly. (to **plane**)
e) The electrician **taped** the wires. (to **tape**)
f) My grandfather **hoped** you would be here. (to **hope**)
g) He was **hoping** to come. (to **hope**)

You see how the final –e in the infinitive **makes the vowel say its name**:

to pl**a**ne	*phonetically*	(pleɪn)
to t**a**pe	*phonetically*	(teɪp)
to h**o**pe	*phonetically*	(haʊp).

In the one-one-one words, the vowels **say their sound**:

to pl**a**n	*phonetically*	(plæn)
to t**a**p	*phonetically*	(tæp)
to h**o**p	*phonetically*	(hɒp).

You never have to double a consonant in a magic –e word. The problem is whether to retain or drop the final –e of the word.

Look at these combinations carefully.

spite + ful	**spite**ful	believ¢ + er	**believer**
sincere + ly	**sincere**ly	declar¢ + ation	**declaration**

34

achieve + ment	**achieve**ment	tak$\not e$ + ing	**tak**ing
feeble + ness	**feeble**ness	craz$\not e$ + y	**craz**y
some + thing	**some**thing	defin$\not e$ + ition	**defin**ition
safe + ty	**safe**ty	desir$\not e$ + able	**desir**able

We can formulate the rule as follows.

Rule 7

Keep the –e when adding a **consonant** suffix to a magic –e word. (**K**eep with a **c**onsonant . . .)

like + ly = lik**e**ly

Drop the –e when adding a **vowel** suffix to a magic –e word.

lik$\not e$ + ing = liking

EXERCISE 22

Join these consonant suffixes to the base words.

1) love + ly   4) some + thing

2) care + ful   5) white + ness

3) arrange + ment

EXERCISE 23

Join these vowel suffixes to the base words.

1) love + ing   4) admire + able

2) participate + ion 5) ignore + ance

3) wave + y

EXERCISE 24

Join suffixes to base words. Try not to look back at the rule, once you've made sure you understand it.

1) immense + ly
2) pine + ing
3) use + ful
4) separate + ly
5) umpire + ing

6) examine + ation
7) expense + ive
8) laze + y
9) trite + ness
10) definite + ly

EXERCISE 25

Try one more exercise before I deal with the very few exceptions to Rule 7. Do your best to get full marks. This is a very important rule that affects thousands of words.

1) The class was (make + ing) a dreadful noise.
2) There is a tremendous (improve + ment) in your work.
3) I wish you would try (breathe + ing) through your nose.
4) The new assistant's legs were (ache + ing) by lunchtime.
5) Amelia's (excite + ment) was intense as the curtain went up.
6) The wedding (prepare + ations) are all complete.
7) They are (share + ing) the cost between them.
8) The old man's (devote + ion) to his dog was very touching.

9) I thought he spoke very (sincere + ly).

10) Were you (nerve + ous) singing in front of so many people?

- **Exceptions to Rule 7**   The few exceptions fall into four categories.

    1) The –e is dropped in eight words before a **consonant** suffix:

whilst	truly	argument
wisdom	duly	wholly
	ninth	awful.

    Remember: WHILST his WISDOM is now in doubt, TRULY and DULY, his NINTH ARGUMENT is WHOLLY AWFUL.

    2) The –e is retained before a **vowel** suffix in words like:

gorgeous	manageable
courageous	noticeable.

    The reason for this is to make sure the g continues to sound like j and the c continues to sound like s. They stay soft like this if they are followed by i or e. They sound hard if they are followed by a, o, u as they would otherwise be here. (Compare cat and got
    cut and gut.)

3) The –e is retained in these words to avoid confusion:

dyeing is different from dying
singeing is different from singing, etc.

These words look more familiar with –e:

ageing	shoeing
mileage	toeing
queueing	hoeing
	canoeing, etc.

Note judgement *or* judgment

acknowledgement *or* acknowledgment

4) A few words ending in **–ce** change to **–ci–** before –ous and –al, such as:

v**ice** vi**ci**ous **race** ra**ci**al.

EXERCISE 26

In the following sentences, add the suffixes as before to the base words, but be on your guard for exceptions to this rule.

1) It's no use (argue + ing) about it.

2) The (renovate + ion) is long overdue.

3) You very (wise + ly) remained silent.

4) Kenny Everett's humour is quite (outrage + ous).

5) (Time + ing) is very important.

6) The two cats were (hope + ing) for an early tea.

7) I am (true + ly) sorry.

8) That pencil case was her (nine + th) this year.

9) The (dine + ing) room has been redecorated.

10) Can you give me (arrive + al) and departure times, please?

11) He's a professional (dive + er) in the Orkneys.

12) The broken part is (replace + able).

13) Your (write + ing) is much easier to read now.

14) I'm not very (hope + ful) about my chances.

15) Use 'Yours (sincere + ly)' at the end of the letter if you start the letter 'Dear Mr Brown'.

As you will have noticed, there may not be many exceptions to Rule 7 but there are some very commonly used words among them! It's really worth learning them by heart if you can.

Revision exercises based on Rules 6 and 7

EXERCISE 27

So many spelling errors arise from confusion between **one-one-one** words and **magic –e** words that I would like you to have a chance of testing your grasp of Rules 6 and 7. Read the rules through again if you wish before doing the following exercise from memory by correctly adding the suffix to the base word.

1) We were (hope + ing) the sun would shine.

2) The men (rob + ing) the bank were caught in the act.

3) Try (hop + ing) twenty times up and down the path.

4) They siphoned off the petrol with some plastic (tube + ing).

5) Class 3 will visit the (can + ing) factory next term.

6) The wicked fairy was (bide + ing) her time.

7) The lad was (shin + ing) up the greasy pole.

8) Sophie, you're (slop + ing) the water everywhere!

9) I am glad that (cane + ing) has been abolished.

10) The poor dog is (pine + ing) for his master.

11) Petronella's bedroom had a (slope + ing) ceiling.

12) Henry and Ricky were (plan + ing) their holiday.

13) Mary was (pin + ing) up the hem at the time.

14) Don't stand so close when I am (plane + ing) wood.

15) The sun was (shine + ing) brightly by ten o'clock.

EXERCISE 28

In pairs, decide from which infinitive each of these words has come.

Example **Q:** pinning   **A:** to pin

1) siting
2) batting
3) shamming
4) caning
5) snipping
6) rating
7) rapping
8) robing
9) mating
10) taping

EXERCISE 29

All the words in this exercise have been used in the previous two exercises. In pairs, can you read them aloud to your partner without hesitation and without making a mistake? See how many attempts it takes.

1) shining	10) hoping
2) shinning	11) tubing
3) pinning	12) robbing
4) pining	13) biding
5) planing	14) sloping
6) planning	15) slopping
7) hopping	16) canning
8) robing	17) caning
9) taping	18) shamming

EXERCISE 30

Prepared Dictation

As the Easter holidays approached, conscientious students began revising in earnest, but others let the opportunity for such sensible systematic preparations pass by, even though the future careers of some of them depended largely on their examination results. Ever hopeful, they trusted to luck and the inspiration of the moment. The period for congratulations or commiserations was safely distant and they had no intention of sacrificing their leisure time.

SPELLING HAZARDS

1) approached   2) conscientious

41

3) earnest 7) period
4) opportunity 8) intention
5) careers 9) sacrificing
6) moment 10) leisure

The –Y rule expanded

In Chapter One we looked at the way that nouns ending in –y form their plurals (Rule 3). This rule is really a wider application of that pattern.

Look carefully at the following two boxes and see how once again the base words ending in vowel +y are much more straightforward than those ending in a consonant +y.

employ	**employ**ing	**employ**ment
enjoy	**enjoy**ing	**enjoy**ment
pay	**pay**ing	**pay**ment
play	**play**ing	**play**ful

beau**ty**	beautiful
ear**ly**	earlier
hea**vy**	heavier
bu**sy**	business

We can formulate the rule right away.

Rule 8

If the base word ends in a **vowel +y**, just add vowel or consonant suffixes.

   empl**oy**   **employ**ing   **employ**ment

If the base word ends in a **consonant +y**, change **y** to **i** before adding suffix.

         beau**ty**   beautiful
         ear**ly**   earlier

● You don't have to change **y** to **i** if the vowel suffix begins with i already

   try tri**ed** (but trying)
   cry cri**ed** (but crying)

A double i would look very ugly.

Remember that this rule follows exactly the same pattern as the rule for the plural of words ending in –y. Just as <u>boy</u> became <u>boys</u> so now <u>enjoy</u> becomes <u>enjoying</u> and <u>enjoyment</u>. Remember also that it makes no difference whether the suffix is a vowel or a consonant one. The vital factor is the ending of the base word.

EXERCISE 31

Complete the following advertising punchlines.

1) **Zanussi**, the (apply + ance) of science.

2) **Boots** best buys for the body (beauty + ful).

3) With one of our Part Exchange Schemes you could be (enjoy + ing) life in a brand-new **McCarthy & Stone** apartment in next to no time.

4) If you're looking to lead a (healthy + er) lifestyle, try new **Hermesetas Light** in the bright modern packs.

5) In fact, **Waistline** is not only preferred for its taste but also for its smooth (creamy + ness) and consistency.

6) To get out stains like these, as (easy + ly) as this, simply get out the **Bio-tex**.

7) First time buyers are in for a pleasant surprise at the **Woolwich**. The Woolwich First Timers' Mortgage. It offers you 1 per cent p.a. off our normal endowment rate (vary + able) for one year giving a current rate of 14.25 per cent (15.4 per cent typical APR vary + able).

8) To the retailer: ICI Paints will redeem this coupon at face value plus normal trade handling allowance provided *only* that it has been taken as part (pay + ment) for a 2.5 litre can of Kitchens & Emulsions from **Dulux**.

9) The seven seater model redefines the term 'people (carry + er)'; providing more than enough room for seven adults, and with folding seats, an endless variety of space options. The **Nissan Prairie** – as good-looking around town as it is practical in the country.

10) Abraham Lincoln, Marco Polo. Even old Juan Carlos. They're all (family + ar) faces down at **Thomas Cook**.

EXERCISE 32

Two-minute brainteaser

Match base words with suffixes. Remember that **each suffix can be used once only** and you should aim to provide a suitable suffix for each of the base words in the two minutes provided. Words must be spelt correctly!

Base words		Suffixes	
1) empty	6) penny	–ance	–or
2) deny	7) forty	–er	–ous
3) ally	8) survey	–ing	–eth
4) study	9) plenty	–less	–al
5) pray	10) destroy	–ed	–ful

EXERCISE 33

In pairs decide why there is no change to the –y of the base words when combined with these suffixes. Remember there are **two** possible reasons.

1) fly + ing

2) bray + ed

3) apply + ing

4) slay + ing

5) delay + ed

6) pay + ee

7) petrify + ing

8) volley + ing

9) annoy + ance

10) empty + ing

- **Exceptions** These eleven words are irregular. The first four (laid, paid, said, daily) are very high-frequency words (you will use them frequently) and so you should learn them by heart.

lay	**laid (mislaid)**
pay	**paid (repaid** etc.) (*but* payer, payee, payment)
day	**daily**
say	**said**
gay	**gaily (gaiety)**
slay	**slain** (but slayer is regular)
dry	**dryness, dryly**
shy	**shyness, shyly**
sly	**slyness, slyly**
wry	**wryness, wryly**
baby	**babyhood**

BEWARE
EXCEPTIONS

EXERCISE 34

Test your understanding of Rule 8 and the eleven exceptions.

1) The children were seen (hurry + ing) down the road.

2) I shall never forget her (lovely + ness) that evening.

3) Stephen packed his case in (ready + ness) for the journey.

4) The Chairman apologised for having (mislay + ed) his notes.

5) The clergyman (pity + ed) the poor soul with all his heart.

6) I (envy + ed) her willingness and energy!

7) I was sure John had (copy + ed) Robert's work.

8) (Day + ly) she lit the fire at 6.00 a.m.

9) There was a (dry + ness) in Mrs Norman's throat as she thanked the girls for the last time.

10) Her husband (try + ed) to erect the tent by himself but failed dismally.

11) The unknown knight (parry + ed) all his blows (easy + ly).

12) Who (supply + ed) the tools?

13) They (say + ed) they were not coming.

14) His footsteps rang mournfully in the echoing (empty + ness) of the hospital corridors.

EXERCISE 34

Prepared Dictation

Sheila Brown was a trainee <u>librarian</u>. She <u>enjoyed</u> the work immensely despite her <u>shyness</u>. She <u>said</u> a few appropriate words of greeting to all who came to the library. Some pensioners arrived <u>daily</u> to read the newspapers and temporarily ease the <u>loneliness</u> of their lives. The Reference Library was always full of college students, writing and reading <u>steadily</u>. She was <u>busiest</u> of all on Saturdays when whole families changed their books. She would recommend <u>librarianship</u> as a career enthusiastically to anyone who loved books and was intelligent and methodical.

1) imm**e**ns**e**ly (magic –e word)   2) app**ro**priate

3) arrived

4) temporarily

5) reference

6) library

7) college

8) recommend

9) enthusiastically

10) intelligent

Two-one-one words

This is a very useful rule (which many people are regularly grateful for). It sounds rather complicated because you have to say the word to yourself and see whether the first or the second syllable is stressed before you can apply the rule. Once you understand it, it's with you for life; so do persevere.

It's called the **two-one-one rule** because it applies to words with two syllables which have one final consonant preceded by one vowel.

Consider these two words.

gallop	he gallops	he is galloping
begin	she begins	she is beginning

Both 'gallop' and 'begin' are two-one-one words. Both base words remain unchanged when the consonant **s** is added; gallop doesn't double its final consonant when a vowel suffix is added; begin does. Why?

It's not so arbitrary as it looks because there is an important difference between the stress in the word 'gallop' and the stress in the word 'begin'. If you exaggerate the stress, you will see you emphasise the first syllable in one (GALLop) and the second syllable in the other (beGIN).

Rule 9

There is **no change** to a two-one-one base word when a **consonant** suffix is added.

allot	**allot**ment	**number**	**number**less
forget	**forget**ful	**tender**	**tender**ness

Take care when adding a **vowel** suffix.

a) If the stress is on the <u>first</u> syllable, have <u>one</u> consonant when adding suffix.

    ORbit   orbited   orbiting
    FASTen   fastened   fastening

b) If the stress is on the <u>second</u> syllable, have <u>two</u> consonants when adding suffix.

    oc**CUR**   occurred   occurring
    sub**MIT**   submitted   submitting

● Remember the rule for adding vowel syllables using numbers:

1st   syllable stressed, use **1** consonant
2nd syllable stressed, use **2** consonants.

Clearly the application of this rule will depend on your ability to determine which syllable of a two-one-one word is stressed. You may find it helpful to incorporate the word into a sentence and to try stressing first one syllable and then the other.

If your ear does not help you, your dictionary will. The main accent will be shown by this mark ' placed either *after* the stressed syllable (GALLop is shown as gall'op) or, in some dictionaries, *before* the stressed syllable (GALLop is shown as 'gallop).

GALL OP ING

Don't be confused by the different symbols positioned over the vowels; these help with pronunciation, not stress.

Read the following ten words aloud to yourself. Exaggerate the stress. Can you see that the stress is on the first syllable of each word? (In other words, you say it more heavily.)

pivot	hamper
alter	orbit
number	offer
lengthen	gallop
market	budget

In the following words, the stress is on the second syllable. Read them aloud, exaggerating the stress, so that you are quite clear what is meant.

forbid	recur
outwit	begin
regret	compel
propel	outbid
permit (verb)	admit

Notice the <u>verb</u> **permit** is **permit** with the stress on the second syllable. The <u>noun</u> **permit** has the stress on the first syllable. There are other words like this.

EXERCISE 36

Pronounce these words and decide where the stress comes.

1) omit	11) transmit
2) limit	12) worship
3) impel	13) submit
4) differ	14) travel
5) occur	15) appal
6) hasten	16) quarrel
7) commit	17) patrol
8) label	18) profit
9) prefer	19) debar
10) fasten	20) packet

Here the even numbers have the stress on the first syllable and the odd numbers have the stress on the second.

EXERCISE 37

Decide where the stress comes by pronouncing these words.

1) hinder	9) cancel
2) acquit	10) defer
3) enter	11) signal
4) equip	12) infer
5) happen	13) rivet
6) excel	14) expel
7) suffer	15) peter
8) annul	16) prefer

Now the even numbers have the stress on the second syllable and it is the odd numbers that have the stress on the first.

If you're quite confident about deciding which of the two syllables in two-one-one words is stressed, then try the next exercise. Read the rule again. Remember it's only when adding vowel suffixes that you have to decide whether to double final consonants or not.

EXERCISE 38

Complete the following.

1) limit + ing
2) profit + able
3) worship + ful
4) commit + al
5) admit + ing
6) alter + ation
7) equip + ing
8) equip + ment
9) forbid + en
10) market + ing

Don't worry if you are making mistakes at this stage. Look again at the rule and try the following exercises with a partner.

EXERCISE 39

In pairs, complete the following.

1) begin + er
2) allot + ment
3) forget + ing
4) forget + ful
5) limit + less
6) omit + ing
7) listen + ing
8) gossip + ed
9) acquit+ ed
10) regret + ed

EXERCISE 40

In pairs, do your best to score 100% with this exercise. Add suffixes to the two-one-one base words as indicated.

1) Am I (permit + ed) to smoke?

2) They enjoy (garden + ing) very much.

3) The enterprise was a (profit + able) one.

4) The Prince of Wales (pilot + ed) the plane.

5) I am afraid your days as Chairman are (number + ed).

6) Your aunt has bought you a (digit + al) watch.

7) The little boy (outwit + ed) both parents.

8) The astronauts have (orbit + ed) Venus.

9) (Packet + ed) biscuits always cost more.

10) My husband (order + ed) me to wash up. I refused.

11) The house will be quieter when the rooms are (carpet + ed) .

12) The neighbours have been (gossip + ing) again.

13) Nathan (submit + ed) reluctantly to a dental inspection.

14) The programme on badgers will be (transmit + ed) at the weekend.

15) The boulder was (lever + ed) into position.

16) After a few yards the path (peter + ed) out.

17) You were (hammer + ing) into the early hours.

18) You should make allowances. He is a (begin + er).

19) Those accounts must be (audit + ed).

20) I am glad to say the poor lad has been (acquit + ed).

There is a **change of stress** in the following words and so sometimes the final consonant of the base word is doubled, sometimes it is not.

con**fer**	con**ferr**ed	con**ferr**ing	**con**ference
de**fer**	de**ferr**ed	de**ferr**ing	**def**erence
pre**fer**	pre**ferr**ed	pre**ferr**ing	**pref**erence
re**fer**	re**ferr**ed	re**ferr**ing	**ref**erence
trans**fer**	trans**ferr**ed	trans**ferr**ing	**trans**ference

Stress on 2nd syllable, double **r**

Stress on 1st syllable, single **r**

BEWARE
EXCEPTIONS

● **Exceptions to Rule 9** There are three groups of words to look out for.

1) These **never** double whatever the stress: words ending in **w**, **x** and **y** because they would look so odd. So we have: allo**w**ed, rela**x**ed, betra**y**ed.

2) These **always** double whatever the stress: **worship**, **kidnap**, **outfit** and **handicap** (actually three syllables but usefully included here). So we have: worshi**pp**ed, kidna**pp**ed, outfi**tt**er and handica**pp**ed.

3) These **sometimes** double, irrespective of stress, but depending which vowel suffix is being used:

Words ending in **l** double the letter before most vowel suffixes (quarre**ll**ing, annu**ll**ed, cance**ll**ation, propeller) but they never double before –ity, –ise or –ize (formality, civility, legalise, penalise).

However, learn para<u>ll</u>e<u>lo</u>g<u>r</u>am!

The exceptions are a nuisance but I'm still grateful for the rule. Most of the exceptions are no trouble anyway. It's the words ending in l that are likely to cause trouble. Just remember that **l is a special case** and be prepared to look those up.

Remember that [L] is a special case!

EXERCISE 41

This exercise involves base words ending in l. See how you get on.

1) I very much regret the (cancel + ation) of the Shadows' concert.

2) Michael was (pedal + ing) furiously up the hill.

3) You've always been a (quarrel + some) child.

4) What an (appal + ing) tragedy!

5) You could help by (label + ing) the bottles.

6) He's buying his motorbike by (instal + ments).

7) He's buying his motorbike by (install + ments). (Alternative spelling.)

8) What (propel + ant) is used in that aerosol?

9) Late-night (revel + ers) kept us awake most of the night.

10) Your grasp of this rule is (excel + ent).

EXERCISE 42
Spelling Quiz on Two-one-one Words

Prepare the answers individually first, looking back at rules and exceptions, and referring to spelling note-books and dictionaries. Then divide into teams as outlined in Exercise 5 on page 8. Members of the winning team will probably have the confidence to risk answering questions without conferring but the possi-bility of conferring remains.

Join base word with suffix.

1) marvel + ous
2) omit + ed
3) compel + ed
4) rivet + ed
5) prefer + ence
6) forbid + en
7) commit + ment
8) profit + able
9) gallop + ed
10) patrol + ed
11) travel + ing
12) fasten + ing
13) limit + less
14) quarrel + some
15) equip + ed
16) label + ed
17) market + able
18) expel + ed
19) inter + ment
20) debar + ed
21) worship + ing
22) equip + ment
23) pivot + ing
24) budget + ed

25)	differ + ent	32)	ballot + ed
26)	occur + ence	33)	civil + ise
27)	sandal + ed	34)	pilot + ed
28)	begin + er	35)	admit + ance
29)	regret + ful	36)	prefer + ed
30)	chirrup + ing	37)	annul + ment
31)	hamper + ing	38)	profit + ed

EXERCISE 43

Prepared Dictation

We searched for accommodation in the village for months before <u>finally</u> buying our tiny thatched cottage. We worked hard the first autumn at structural <u>alterations</u> and redecoration and by Easter it was <u>papered</u> and painted, furnished and <u>carpeted</u>. It looked <u>marvellous</u>, so <u>different</u> from the dingy, drab little house that had been neglected for years. We've never <u>regretted</u> our decision to buy it although interest rates were <u>beginning</u> to rise at the time and we needed a colossal mortgage. A house is an <u>excellent</u> investment and, although we have no immediate intention of selling, we know we have a very <u>marketable</u> commodity.

SPELLING HAZARDS

1) sear**ch**ed
2) accom**m**odation
3) din**gy**
4) de**ci**sion
5) int**e**rest

6) colo**ss**al
7) mor**t**gage
8) **immed**iate
9) inten**t**ion
10) com**m**odity

EXERCISE 44

Revise all four rules in this chapter by completing the words in brackets. There are four one-one-one words, seven two-one-one words, four words where you have to apply the –Y rule expanded and ten magic –e words.

FRICTION ACROSS THE FENCE

Neighbours by Hugh Thompson

Twice a week, the soap opera 'Neighbours' has more than 16m Britons glued to the goings-on in Ramsay Street, Melbourne. Closer to home (equal + ly) large audiences follow the activities in Albert Square ('EastEnders'), Coronation Street and Brookside Close. The scripts peddle a fantasy of everyday life in (sun + y) suburb or (grit + y) inner city based on warm relationships and (communicate + ion) on many levels. But the real world is (differ + ent).

Surveys show that 80% feel their neighbours are inconsiderate, 25% don't talk to them, and 10% don't even know their names. One million householders in the UK would like to move because of the people next door.

The (big + est) causes of friction are noise, car parking, fences and the old complaining about the young. With increases in car and home (owner + ship), the percentage of pensioners in the (populate + ation) and the power of music systems, there is little (likely + hood) of any let-up.

Latest figures from the Institute of Environmental

Health Officers, who are most directly in the (fire + ing) line, show that over a 10-year period 'incidents of domestic nuisance' have gone up more than 13 times. In Islington, North London, it has been (calculate + ed) that a third of recorded violence starts with an (argue + ment) between neighbours.

Geoff Fish, chief environmental health officer in Barnet, North London says: 'The noise complaints are on the increase. With all our machines we are getting (noisy + er), more and more live in flats and divided houses often protected by a thin party wall which is in no way (equip + ed) to handle 60-watt stereos or the noise of tumble-(dry + ers).

However, in many cases the councils, police, courts and (house + ing) officers who receive the bulk of the more serious complaints are (power + less) – and not all that prepared to deal with what are often trivial and deeply personal cases. Some solution is (come + ing) from the (mediate + ion) centres which are springing up around the country.

Research by the Policy Studies Institute shows that where neighbours become friends they provide help with the children, (shop + ing), DIY, looking after the home and (person + al) advice.

But, (unhappy + ly), its survey also showed that 90% of neighbours had never shared a meal, 80% had never had a drink together and 20% had never even (offer + ed) each other a cup of tea.

With that degree of (isolate + ion), it is hardly (surprise + ing) that disputes are on the increase.

The Sunday Times, 11 June 1989 (abridged)
© Times Newspapers Ltd 1989

EXERCISE 45

This is a revision test on all the words in the cautionary lists accompanying the prepared dictation exercises in this chapter. Ask someone to dictate them to you.

1) decided
2) volunteered
3) finished
4) approached
5) sacrificing
6) arrived
7) recommend
8) searched
9) immensely
10) temporarily
11) enthusiastically
12) neighbour
13) niece
14) surprise
15) opportunity
16) careers
17) moment
18) period
19) intention
20) leisure

21) reference
22) library
23) college
24) accommodation
25) decision
26) interest
27) mortgage
28) intention
29) commodity
30) woollen
31) awkward
32) pleasant
33) familiar
34) conscientious
35) earnest
36) appropriate
37) intelligent
38) dingy
39) colossal
40) immediate

Before leaving suffixes, we ought just to look at a few that can cause trouble because they are easily confused.

There are some generalisations which can be useful guide-lines.

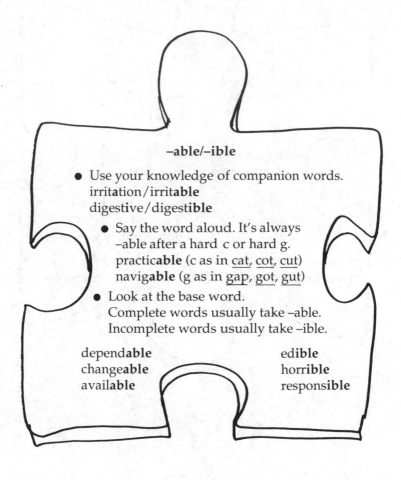

–able/–ible

- Use your knowledge of companion words.
  irrita**tion**/irrit**able**
  diges**tive**/diges**tible**

  - Say the word aloud. It's always
    –able after a hard c or hard g.
    practic**able** (c as in <u>c</u>at, <u>c</u>ot, <u>c</u>ut)
    navig**able** (g as in <u>g</u>ap, <u>g</u>ot, <u>g</u>ut)

- Look at the base word.
  Complete words usually take –able.
  Incomplete words usually take –ible.

depend**able**   ed**ible**
change**able**   horr**ible**
avail**able**   respons**ible**

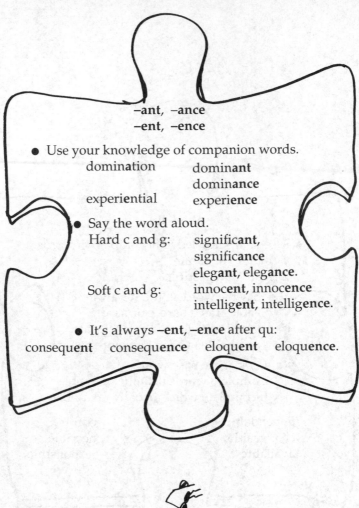

–ant, –ance
–ent, –ence

- Use your knowledge of companion words.

  domination   dominant
                         dominance

  experiential   experience

- Say the word aloud.

  Hard c and g: significant,
                         significance
                         elegant, elegance.

  Soft c and g: innocent, innocence
                         intelligent, intelligence.

- It's always **–ent, –ence** after qu:

  consequent   consequence   eloquent   eloquence.

eleg<u>ant</u>

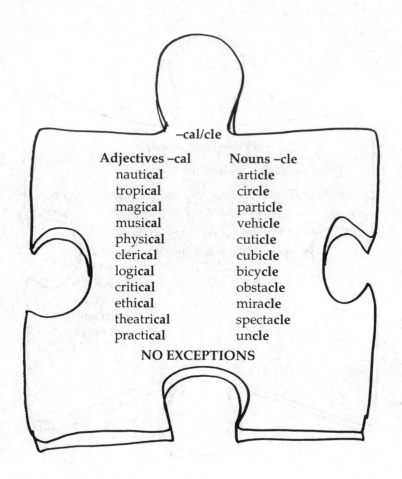

–cal/cle

Adjectives –cal	Nouns –cle
nautical	article
tropical	circle
magical	particle
musical	vehicle
physical	cuticle
clerical	cubicle
logical	bicycle
critical	obstacle
ethical	miracle
theatrical	spectacle
practical	uncle

NO EXCEPTIONS

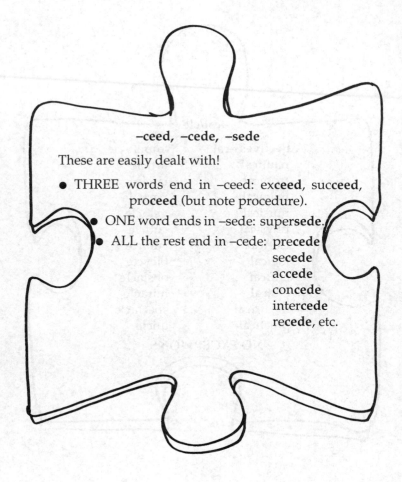

–ceed, –cede, –sede

These are easily dealt with!

- THREE words end in –ceed: ex**ceed**, suc**ceed**, pro**ceed** (but note procedure).
- ONE word ends in –sede: super**sede**.
- ALL the rest end in –cede: pre**cede**
  se**cede**
  ac**cede**
  con**cede**
  inter**cede**
  re**cede**, etc.

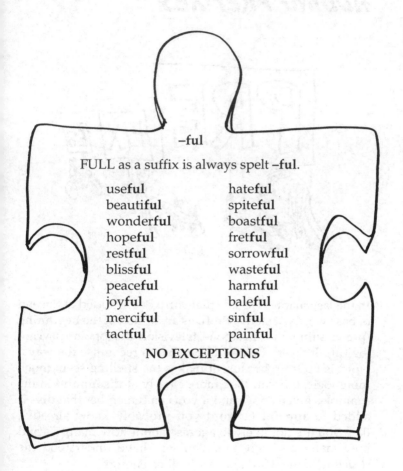

–ful

FULL as a suffix is always spelt **–ful**.

use**ful**	hate**ful**
beaut**iful**	spite**ful**
wonder**ful**	boast**ful**
hope**ful**	fret**ful**
rest**ful**	sorrow**ful**
bliss**ful**	waste**ful**
peace**ful**	harm**ful**
joy**ful**	bale**ful**
merci**ful**	sin**ful**
tact**ful**	pain**ful**

NO EXCEPTIONS

Chapter Three

ADDING PREFIXES

In the last chapter we saw that suffixes are added at the end of base words or stems. **Prefixes** are added at the **beginning** (**pre**fix, **sub**marine, **post**pone, **tele**vision, **dis**appoint, **psycho-**logical). It's very helpful to be able to recognise the way a word is built up because it makes the spelling seem much more logical. If you look more closely at **disappoint** in the examples given above and if you can remember that **dis–** is added to **appoint** (a word you probably know already), then you are not likely to agonise about how many s's and how many p's there are. You will have understood the *structure* of the word and that will be enough.

Some prefixes like **psych–**, **chrono–**, **peri–**, **mega–** can look very complicated when combined with a base word or stem and so it will be helpful to isolate the prefixes for a little while and have a good look at them so that you can spell that part of the word with every confidence.

Common prefixes

Here is a list of frequently used prefixes. Remember how much a dictionary can tell you about a word. A good dictionary tells you not only the meaning of a word, its spelling and its pronunciation, but also its derivation. Study the derivation of a word when you look it up in the dictionary. You will then see that it is part of a family of words and your familiarity with one member will serve as an introduction to the rest of the family.

The spelling of prefixes marked * can change a little as we shall see later.

asleep (Anglo-Saxon <u>on</u>, <u>in</u>)
avert, **ab**sent (Latin <u>away</u>)
***ad**vent (Latin <u>to</u>)
ante-natal (Latin <u>before</u>)
antidote (Greek <u>against</u>)
archbishop (Greek <u>chief</u>)
autograph (Greek <u>self</u>)
benevolent (Latin <u>well</u>)
bicycle (Latin <u>two</u>)
circumference (Latin <u>around</u>)
chronological (Greek <u>time</u>)
***con**nect (Latin <u>with</u>)
contradict (Latin <u>against</u>)
dethrone (Latin <u>down</u>, <u>from</u>)
***dis**integrate (Latin <u>apart</u>)
exit (Latin <u>out</u>)
extraordinary (Latin <u>beyond</u>)
forecast (Old English <u>beforehand</u>)
hemisphere (Greek <u>half</u>)
heterosexual (Greek <u>other</u>)
homosexual (Greek <u>same</u>)
hydro-electric (Greek <u>water</u>)
hyperactive (Greek <u>over much</u>)
hypocrite (Greek <u>under</u>)

*incapable (Latin not)
interview (Latin between)
intravenous (Latin within)
introvert (Latin to the inside)
malevolent (Latin evil)
manual (Latin hand)
megaphone (Greek great)
microscope (Greek small)
misunderstanding (Old English wrongly)
monotonous (Greek single)
multitude (Latin many)
nonsense (Latin not)
obstruct (Latin in the way of)
orthodontist (Greek straight)
panorama (Greek all)
parallel (Greek by the side of)
persevere (Latin through)
perimeter (Greek round/about))
photograpy (Greek light)
polygamy (Greek many)
postpone (Latin after)
prevent (Latin before)
prototype (Greek first)
psychology (Greek soul, mind)
quadruped (Latin four)
revise (Latin again)
retrograde (Latin backwards)
semicircle (Latin half)
*submarine (Latin under)
supercilious (Latin above)
synchronise (Latin together)
television (Greek far off)
thermometer (Greek heat)
transfer (Latin across)
triangle (Latin three)
unsympathetic (Old English not)
vice-captain (Latin in place of)
withstand (Old English against)

EXERCISE 46

Using your dictionary for reference, explain the meaning of these prefixes. Remember you can look up the prefix on its own in most dictionaries as well as the complete word.

1) **omni**potent
2) **holi**day
3) **magni**ficent
4) **micro**scopic
5) **bureau**cratic
6) **ophthalmo**logy
7) **meta**morphosis
8) **pen**ultimate
9) **se**cluded
10) **pedi**cure

11) **vivi**section
12) **legi**slate
13) **phil**anthropist
14) **ne**glect
15) **bio**logy
16) **for**bid
17) **haemo**rrhage
18) **demo**cracy
19) **pseudo**nym
20) **co**-operate

You will find that your spelling will improve rapidly as you begin to look closely at words and take an interest in their structure and derivation. A good dictionary is a necessity. If you haven't got a dictionary already, do decide to treat yourself to one. Look at the ones displayed in a good bookshop and take your time over your choice. Look up the same words in several editions and see how much information each gives. Pay attention also to layout and typeface because some dictionaries are far more welcoming than others and are easier to use. Buy the very best you can afford. You will find a good dictionary is a really good investment. It will last you for years.

The five chameleons

Just as chameleons take on the colour of their surroundings, so prefixes can change their final letter to the initial letter of the word they're combined with (or sometimes to another letter that sounds pleasing with it). As a result, the word becomes much easier to say. Here are some examples.

AD– changes before **c, f, g, l, m, n, p, q, r, s, t**.
accuse
affect
aggravate
allocate
ammunition
announce
appear
acquire
arrange
assemble
attend

CON– changes before **h, l, b, m, p, r**, and **some vowels**.
cohere
collect
combine
community
compose
correct
co-operate

DIS– changes before **f**.
different

IN– changes before **b, l, m, p, r**.
imbibe
illiterate
immature

impossible
irregular
and notice **ig**nore

SUB– changes before **c, f, g, m, p, r.**
succeed
suffix
suggest
summon
suppose
surrogate

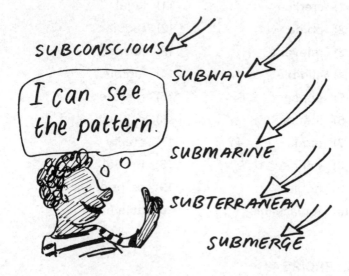

There's certainly no need to learn all this by heart but be <u>aware</u> of what is happening to the spelling of a prefix. When a prefix changes its final letter to match the initial letter or the word it's being combined with, you have a double letter which then becomes logical to you when you spell it. You can see the pattern and 'seeing the pattern' is the basis for good spelling.

Be aware too of the need for a **double letter** if the **final letter** of the prefix is already the same as the **initial letter** of the words it is joining.

disappoint   **dis**ingenuous   **dis**quiet
but
dissatisfy   **dis**semination   **dis**solve
misspelling   **with**hold   **under**rate

EXERCISE 47

Form the opposites of these words by using a prefix.

1) credit
2) polite
3) relevant
4) eligible
5) appear
6) literate
7) pious
8) definite
9) noble
10) replaceable

11) legal
12) regular
13) formal
14) legible
15) mature
16) sophisticated
17) ability
18) mortal
19) responsible
20) active

EXERCISE 48

Use an appropriate prefix to complete the following.

1) Try to dispel your ____judices.

2) I should like you to sit in a ____circle facing me.

3) The sky became very ____cast.

4) We shall ____come our enemy.

5) The headmaster was seriously ____pleased.

6) Sebastian spoke his thoughts __loud.

7) It is too late now to __vert disaster.

8) We were ____appointed when the parcel didn't arrive.

9) The small boat ran __ground.

10) How ____hevelled your hair looks.

11) Both girls will come __though they are tired.

12) The Bank will ____hold payment of the cheque.

13) I noticed three ____spellings in your work.

14) You ____rate his ability.

15) Simon __ways writes an interesting essay.

EXERCISE 49

Explain the difference in meaning between the words in these pairs.

1) hypercritical
   hypocritical

2) forward
   foreword

3) disinterested
   uninterested

4) precede
   proceed

5) antidote
   antedate

EXERCISE 50

Prepared Dictation

There are a lot of prefixes in this passage. I have under-lined ten which need special care.

John's parents are very <u>disappointed</u> with his recent College report. His mathematics <u>assignments</u> are <u>apparently</u> often unfinished, and unless he does <u>something</u> quickly about the <u>illogical</u> and inconsistent arrangement of his work, he will be unsuccessful in the final exams. The English language tutor is similarly uncomplimentary. John's essays are <u>immature</u> and frequently completely <u>irrelevant</u>. They are full of <u>misspellings</u> and his writing is often <u>illegible</u>. They want to see an <u>immediate</u> improvement.

SPELLING HAZARDS

1) par**e**nts

2) rec**e**nt

3) math**e**matics

4) inconsist**e**nt

5) ar**r**angement

6) unsu**cc**essful

7) lang**ua**ge

8) tut**or**

9) simi**l**arly

10) uncompl**i**mentary

Chapter Four

WORDS OFTEN CONFUSED

In our language we have a host of troublesome little words which seem to besiege a student as soon as pen is put to paper. These words come in twos and threes and are confusing either because they sound identical (homophones) or because they sound very similar.

I've known students who have guessed wildly for years, not realising that there is a logical basis to draw on.

I've listed alphabetically below the words which, in my experience, cause students the most difficulty. By each word, I've given a sentence which should guide you to the right choice of word in your own composition.

Those of you who make the mistake of writing <u>alot</u> (as one word) and <u>up stairs</u> (as two words) will find the information in boxes on the way through useful too.

accept	I gladly **accept** your offer.
except	Everyone came **except** Alice.
	(Practice Exercise 65)
affect (verb)	Alcohol will **affect** your asthma.
effect (noun)	The **effect** of the cuts was disastrous.
	(Practice Exercise 51)
all most	They were **all most** helpful.
almost	He **almost** choked to death.
allowed (= permitted)	You are **allowed** to smoke.
aloud	She spoke her thoughts **aloud**.
all ready	Are you **all ready** to go?
already	Have you eaten your lunch **already**?

> **ALL RIGHT** is always TWO WORDS
> Are you feeling **all right**?

all so   They were **all so** happy as they set off.

also   He is **also** a qualified pilot.

all together   We found them **all together**.
altogether   It is **altogether** too difficult.

all ways   These are **all ways** into town.
always   She **always** says that.

> **A LOT** (slang) is always TWO WORDS
> He likes her **a lot**.

any way   I cannot think of **any way** to do it.
anyway   I shall invite him **anyway**.

boarder   She was a weekly **boarder** at Roedean.

border   I shall weed the herbaceous **border** tonight.
There are no longer any **border** controls.

breath (noun)   Take a deep **breath** before you start.
breathe (verb)   Don't **breathe** through your mouth.

> **CANNOT** is written as ONE WORD
> I **cannot** help you, I'm afraid.

clothes (= garments)	We all enjoy wearing new **clothes**.
cloths	You need soft **cloths** for polishing.
	(Practice Exercise 65)
complement (= that which completes)	The ship now has its full **complement**.
compliment (praise)	That is the nicest **compliment** I've ever received! (noun)
	May I **compliment** you on your good taste? (verb)
councillor (someone who sits on the council)	**Councillor** Brown won't get my vote again.
counsellor (= adviser)	Why not discuss your problem with the college **counsellor**?
dairy	She's churning butter in the **dairy**.
diary (= journal)	Do you write in your **diary** every day?
desert (noun)	They drove in convoy over the Sahara **Desert**.
dessert (= pudding)	Would you like apple pie for **dessert**?
heroin	**Heroin** is a drug derived from morphine.
heroine	The **heroine** of the novel is a twenty-year-old shop assistant.

IN FACT is always TWO WORDS
I understand. **In fact**, I think you
have made the right decision.

> **IN FRONT** is always TWO WORDS
> Elizabeth spends hours **in front**
> of the mirror.

its (possessive)	The dog raised **its** paw.
it's (= it is) (= it has)	**It's** a pity you can't come.
	It's been raining all night.
	(Practice Exercises 52 and 64)
knew	I **knew** it would kick.
new	You need a **new** waste-bin.
	(Practice Exercise 65)
know	Do you **know** the answer?
no (= not any)	
(= opposite of YES)	I can offer **no** hope.
	No, I don't want to come.
	(Practice Exercise 65)
licence (**c** for noun)	You need a **licence** to drive a car.
license (**s** for verb)	Is this a **licensed** restaurant?
	(Practice Exercise 53)
lightening (verb – present participle)	Her workload is **lightening** a little.
lightning (noun – goes with thunder)	**Lightning** flashed across the sky.
loose (rhymes with goose)	I have a **loose** tooth.

lose (rhymes with whose)	You'll **lose** that wallet. (Practice Exercises 54 and 64)
of (pronounced ov) **off**	She is the mother **of** five. Keep **off** the grass. (Practice Exercise 65)

past (noun)
    (adjective)
    (preposition)
    (adverb)
	I am fascinated by the **past**.
	He is a **past** pupil of mine.
	She walked straight **past** me.
	They walked **past**.

passed (past tense of verb to pass)	Donna has **passed** her exams. I **passed** you in the corridor. (Practice Exercises 55, 56, 64)
personal **personnel**	It is a **personal** matter. Apply to the **Personnel** Officer.
practice (c for the noun) **practise** (s for the verb)	**Practice** makes perfect. You must **practise** for seven hours. (Practice Exercise 57)

● This is a very tricky pair. If you are not always confident about the noun/verb distinction, there is another way. **Advice/advise** are a pair where you can *hear* the spelling difference. Try substituting advice for practice in the example above. It makes a rough kind of sense and confirms that you are dealing with a noun. Similarly if you substitute advise for practise in the second sentence, you can confirm that you need the verb form. (This tip works for licence/license as well.)

principal (= chief)	My **principal** objection is the expense.
principle (= moral motive, fundamental truth)	I objected on **principle**.

● The head of a college is called the <u>Principal</u> (chief lecturer. Remember 'my **pal**, the Princi**pal**').

quiet (= not noisy)	Please be **quiet** for a moment.
quite	You are really **quite** nice. (<u>Practice Exercise 65</u>)
seam (= joined edges of cloth)	You must sew that **seam** again.
seem	They **seem** not to care. (<u>Practice Exercise 65</u>)
shore	The sea**shore** is fascinating.
sure (= certain)	I am **sure** that he will come.
some times	There are **some times** when life seems difficult.
sometimes	**Sometimes** I go to London.
stationary (= not moving)	The car was **stationary** at the time.
stationery (paper, envelopes etc.)	A station**er** sells **stationery**.
thank you	**Thank you**, I should love to come.
thank-you (adjective)	I've finished all my **thank-you** letters.
their (= belonging to them)	They have lost **their** cat.
there (impersonal construction)	**There** is no hope.
(adverb of place)	He ran here and **there**.

they're (= they are)	**They're** always late.
	(Practice Exercises 58, 59, 64)
to (part of infinitive)	I hope **to** see *Hamlet*.
(preposition)	We walked **to** Berlin.
too (= as well)	Are you coming **too**?
(= excessively)	I am **too** fat.
two (= 2)	It cost **two** pounds.
	(Practice Exercises 60, 61, 64, 65)

UPSTAIRS is always ONE WORD
The cat crept **upstairs**.

---

weather (= climate)	The **weather** is so wintry for Easter.
whether (= if)	I don't know **whether** I can come.
were (rhymes with <u>her</u>)	We **were** very sorry.
where (rhymes with <u>air</u>)	**Where** are you going?
	I know **where** he is.
	The house **where** he lives is beautiful.
	(Practice Exercises 62, 63, 64)
who's (= who is)	**Who's** there?
(= who has)	**Who's** been using my hair drier?
whose	**Whose** book is this?
	She is a writer **whose** books I've always loved.
	(Practice Exercise 65)

your (= belonging to you)	Here's **your** bill, madam.
you're (= you are)	**You're** joking!
	(Practice Exercise 65)

'Here is your bill, madam...'

Exercises on words often confused

EXERCISE 51

affect or effect?

1) What will be the _____ of opening on Sundays?

2) We shall all be _____ed by the change.

3) The _____ of the cuts will be disastrous.

4) One _____ of the closure will be increased costs.

5) Nobody who is _____ed by pollen should work here.

6) Will it _____ you at all?

7) The main _____ of reorganisation was a saving.

8) I wonder how the news will _____ his wife.

9) Sunshine has a relaxing _____ on everyone.

10) He is still suffering from the _____s of imprisonment.

11) Prices generally will be _____ed by the rise in the cost of petrol.

12) The sound _____s were marvellous.

13) It _____s me more than it _____s you.

14) The strike will _____ all manufacturing industries.

15) The _____ of the Chancellor's warning was dramatic.

16) She will bear the _____s of an unhappy childhood all her life.

17) Her father seemed quite un_____ed by the news.

18) What will the _____ be on your business?

19) Nobody will be more _____ed by the change than I.

20) The long-term _____s of the Act cannot yet be known.

EXERCISE 52

its or it's?

1) My watch has lost ____ second-hand.

2) I know ____ too late to ask for help.

3) The cat lazily twitched ____ ear.

4) —— quite clear now.

5) That joke has lost ____ point.

6) Few people really enjoy ____ taste.

7) I'm sorry ____ damaged.

8) ____ been difficult walking with crutches.

9) Do you know ____ origin?

10) ____ easy if you know what you're doing

11) ____ a pity that you weren't here.

12) The dog scratched ____ ear.

13) The pram has lost ____ wheel.

14) ____ handle has come off.

15) ____ an ill-wind that blows nobody any good.

16) ____ been a long time since I saw you.

17) ____ too late now.

18) The gardener trimmed ____ branches.

19) ____ ears are too long.

20) The boy kicked ____ top off.

EXERCISE 53

licence or license?

1) You will need a _____.

2) Have you renewed your television _____?

3) Is it necessary to _____ such premises?

4) The _____ is very expensive.

5) The _____ costs five pounds.

6) You must renew your _____ by 30 June.

7) His _____ has nearly expired.

8) He tore the _____ into two very angrily.

9) We hope we can _____ the club for singing and dancing.

10) A current driving _____ is essential.

84

EXERCISE 54

loose or lose?

1) Don't _____ your cheque-book!

2) My belt is too _____.

3) A tooth is painful when it's _____.

4) You'll _____ that pen.

5) I'm afraid the window-frame is rather _____.

6) You'll _____ your place at College if you don't enrol.

7) This tile feels _____.

8) You'll _____ marks for poor punctuation.

9) The _____ wheels were the cause of the accident.

10) _____ paving stones are dangerous.

11) She is very _____-limbed.

12) The _____ change jangled in his pocket.

13) That buckle is wearing _____.

14) It is easy to _____ his respect.

15) You will _____ your way without a compass.

16) They're at a _____ end in the school holidays.

17) I don't want to _____ your friendship.

18) If you _____ the book, you will have to pay a fine.

19) There is a page _____ in this copy.

20) I am sure he will _____ the case.

EXERCISE 55

passed or past?

1) The sentry _____ the spot every fifteen minutes.

2) It is half _____ four.

3) It is _____ my lunch hour.

4) What is the _____ tense of this verb?

5) He has a mysterious _____.

6) I've _____ your house every day this week.

7) The _____ is over and forgotten.

8) The thief ran _____ the 'phone box.

9) We _____ the parcel from hand to hand.

10) The train rushed _____ the platform.

11) The dog ran _____ the gate.

12) _____ the dairy is a butcher's shop.

13) They _____ him every day.

14) It has _____ six o'clock.

15) It is _____ six o'clock.

16) Have you _____ your father the gravy?

17) I _____ you in the Strand this morning.

18) I shall forget the _____ as quickly as I can.

19) Nobody has _____ this spot for one hour.

20) Creep _____ the front door.

EXERCISE 56

passed or past?

1) The bus _____ me at the top of the road.

2) He sauntered _____ the parked car.

3) I should like to know more about his _____.

4) It is a long way _____ lunch-time.

5) My father _____ me a five-pound note.

6) I can never go _____ a sweet-shop without going in.

7) His _____ record is excellent.

8) They _____ the hat around.

9) We must have _____ you on the way.

10) I have _____ that page already.

11) We are _____ our prime.

12) The nurse _____ the scalpel to the surgeon.

13) You have _____ your examination.

14) Your _____ offences cannot be disregarded.

15) Hop _____ the apple tree and then run back.

16) I've been listening to the serial for the _____ ten weeks.

17) My boyfriend walked straight _____ me.

18) The little boys _____ the sweets around.

19) My _____ successes are forgotten now.

20) They have already _____ the half-way point.

EXERCISE 57

practice or practise?

1) An hour's _____ is not enough.

2) Gymnasts must _____ every day.

3) I wonder if he will _____ what he preaches.

4) Regular _____ is essential.

5) The doctor's _____ was a scattered one.

6) You will be able to do it with _____.

7) In _____ the idea is hopeless.

8) The cast will _____ the dance every day.

9) The little girl loathes her piano _____.

10) _____ standing on your head. It will relax you!

EXERCISE 58

their, there or they're?

1) _____ too ill to come to the party.

2) _____ will be a thunder-storm soon.

3) Have you ever been _____ ?

4) I believe _____ quite well-known.

5) Suddenly _____ was a loud bang.

6) I know _____ sorry for what happened.

7) They have sold _____ house.

8) At last _____ coming.

9) I'll get over _____ at once.

10) Please go _____ and wait for me.

11) _____ is no point in arguing.

12) My parents have redecorated _____ kitchen.

13) I've never been _____ before.

14) _____ is no smoke without fire.

15) _____ children are all brilliant.

16) Nobody _____ has ever heard of him.

17) _____ is no point in discussing it.

18) Mrs Greenham is _____ godmother.

19) _____ grandmother was a real character.

20) I know _____ hoping for a visit.

EXERCISE 59

their, there, they're?

1) _____ both very sensible.

2) I know _____ mother will be horrified.

3) I love receiving _____ letters.

4) _____ are three possibilities you should consider.

5) I left my bag over _____.

6) _____ answers are always vague.

7) The hikers had lost _____ way.

8) They waited _____ for ten minutes.

9) _____ both coming.

10) _____ will be trouble over this.

11) _____ a nice family.

12) The delegates have made up _____ minds.

13) I know _____ reliable.

14) _____ must have been some mistake.

15) I hope _____ will be an investigation.

16) My neighbours have cancelled _____ papers.

17) _____ always the first to arrive.

18) Do you know _____ telephone number?

19) I put your sweater _____ myself.

20) Have you seen _____ car?

EXERCISE 60

to, too, two?

1) He wanted _____ go _____ the cinema.

2) It's _____ hot _____ wear a coat.

3) Do you know how _____ do percentages?

4) Maggie hopes _____ 'phone him tomorrow.

5) Will Mrs Jones come _____?

6) These _____ cases are far _____ heavy.

7) Nobody wants _____ be unfair _____ them.

8) Mr Thorne promised _____ give his permission.

9) I _____ enjoy ice-cream.

10) We are _____ excited _____ sleep.

11) _____ young _____ die.

12) _____ cats were seen in the garden.

13) Timothy hopes _____ go _____ University.

14) The shopping bag was _____ flimsy.

15) _____ of us could try _____ contact her.

16) His parents are _____ impatient with him.

17) It's _____ late now.

18) _____ post the parcel will be _____ expensive.

19) He hopes _____ be an architect.

20) No-one is _____ old _____ learn.

EXERCISE 61

to, too, two?

1) It's _____ hot in here.

2) They're _____ stupid _____ change.

3) The whole class is going _____ London by train.

4) I was told _____ leave the room.

5) Is your father coming _____?

6) Will you go _____ the Post Office for me?

7) The headmaster _____ will be in the classroom.

8) Those cats are _____ lazy _____ move.

9) I've never been _____ a foreign country.

10) Do you know how _____ mend a puncture?

11) This cake is _____ rich for me.

12) There are _____ bicycles for sale.

13) You _____ can be a millionaire.

14) _____ heads are better than one.

15) I hope _____ finish this sweater tonight.

16) All their friends laughed _____.

17) Are you allowed _____ eat sweets if you are a diabetic?

18) Nobody likes _____ be criticised all the time.

EXERCISE 62

were or where?

1) _____ did you get that hat?

2) We know _____ you live.

3) The animals _____ shockingly neglected.

4) They _____ very depressed by the news.

5) I know _____ the large plates are.

6) There _____ cobwebs by the sink.

7) _____ is the library?

8) _____ you there?

9) We _____ afraid.

10) Have you any idea _____ we are?

11) I don't know _____ it is.

12) _____ you on the bus?

13) He knows _____ you live.

14) The house _____ the road bends is up for sale.

15) We _____ astonished at the news.

16) They _____ present at the time.

17) I know _____ to find it.

18) The bungalow _____ they live is very tiny.

19) _____ are you?

20) The children _____ running down the road.

EXERCISE 63

were or where?

1) _____ will you live?

2) Do you know _____ my coat is?

3) He hasn't told me _____ he works.

4) _____ you sorry?

5) The staff _____ indignant.

6) We _____ hoping to move to the town _____ my
son lives.

7) The men _____ repairing the road.

8) _____ does it hurt?

9) The workmen _____ wondering _____ to put it.

10) _____ they there?

11) If I _____ you, I'd forget all about it.

12) We stayed in the house _____ Dickens' daughters _____ born.

13) I see now _____ you have been going wrong.

14) I know _____ I would like to go on holiday.

15) All the flags _____ out for the Royal Wedding.

16) That young man knows _____ he wants to go.

17) _____ _____ you on 29 September?

18) _____ are the snows of yester-year?

19) I wonder who the culprits _____ .

20) My neighbours _____ always helpful.

21) _____ you surprised at the news?

EXERCISE 64

Insert appropriate words as indicated.

1) This exercise is _____ difficult for me. (to, too, two)

2) Your _____ experience is valuable to us. (past, passed)

3) _____ you present on the first night? (were, where)

4) They have crashed _____ car. (there, their, they're)

5) _____ have you been since supper? (were, where)

6) I don't want _____ _____ all my teeth. (to, too, two, lose, loose)

7) We _____ horrified at the news. (were, where)

8) Something is _____ in the engine. (lose, loose)

93

9) We will _____ the trail if it starts raining. (lose, loose)

10) _____ never _____ late _____ learn _____ spell. (its, it's, to, too, two)

11) _____ such a pity _____ leaving London. (its, it's, there, their, they're)

12) _____ both hoping for promotion. (there, their, they're)

13) _____ always a race against time in the garden. (its, it's)

14) I _____ old Mr Jones in town this morning. (past, passed)

15) I'm afraid _____ _____ expensive for me. (its, it's, to, too, two)

16) A cat values _____ independence. (its, it's)

17) _____ accuracy cannot be guaranteed. (its, it's)

18) Dr Donald knows _____ parents quite well. (there, their, they're)

19) He has _____ all his papers to me. (past, passed)

EXERCISE 65

Insert the appropriate words as indicated.

1) What beautiful _____ you have! (clothes, cloths)

2) I will give you the best _____ them. (of, off)

3) I was _____ sorry when she left. (quiet, quite)

4) The children went out _____ _____ _____ presents. (to, too, two, buy, by, there, their, they're)

5) Her father _____ all would be well. (new, knew)

6) It would _____ to be a good idea. (seam, seem)

7) Are you _____ _____ you will have time?
(quiet, quite, sure, shore)

8) _____ afraid of Virginia Woolf? (who's, whose)

9) _____ absolutely right. (you're, your)

10) Can you find _____ way through the maze?
(you're, your)

11) I _____ the tour well. (no, know)

12) Please _____ my apologies. (accept, except)

Chapter Five

USEFUL TIPS

In this chapter I want to deal with a number of useful tips and spelling patterns that don't come within the scope of the other unified chapters on plurals, prefixes and suffixes and homophones. Some tips you may know already; others may be new to you.

ie/ei words

Students are often heard chanting the first half of this jingle until they are discouraged by the vast number of exceptions. If you learn the *complete* jingle below, you will have to cope with only **twenty-four** exceptions.

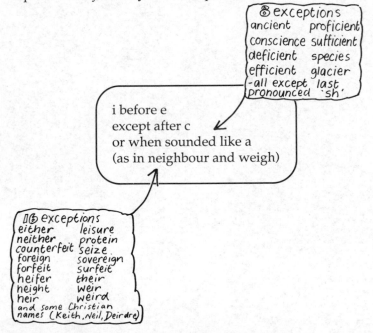

8 exceptions
ancient   proficient
conscience sufficient
deficient   species
efficient   glacier
– all except last
pronounced 'sh'

i before e
except after c
or when sounded like a
(as in neighbour and weigh)

16 exceptions
either   leisure
neither   protein
counterfeit   seize
foreign   sovereign
forfeit   surfeit
heifer   their
height   weir
heir   weird
and some Christian
names (Keith, Neil, Deirdre)

This is my <u>ni</u>ce <u>nie</u>ce, <u>Ni</u>cola..

EXERCISE 66

This is a straightforward exercise where you don't need to worry about exceptions. You will need to use **ie** four times and **ei** six times (twice after c and four times because the vowels sound as if they're spelt a).

1) She held the r__ns lightly.

2) There are __ght spare places on the coach.

3) Everyone must dress as a Caval__r or a Roundhead.

4) I rec__ved your letter on Friday.

5) We are going to buy a golden retr__ver.

6) My nephew is so conc__ted.

7) P__rce the top to let the air out.

8) Prince Charles is h__r to the throne.

9) Do you know th__r address?

10) You've been a very good fr__nd to me.

EXERCISE 67

Try again with another straightforward exercise.

1) perc__ve
2) sk__n
3) dec__t
4) c__ling
5) r__ndeer

6) f__ld
7) gr__ve
8) br__f
9) conc__ve
10) v__l

EXERCISE 68

This time, exceptions are included. Be on your guard!

1) My n__ce will be __ghteen tomorrow.

2) The pr__st spoke seriously to Sh__la.

3) A p__rcing shr__k terrified the aud__nce.

4) My n__ghbour bel__ves the world is flat.

5) Our sover__gn, Queen Elizabeth, has r__gned for forty years.

6) __ght r__ndeer pulled the sl__gh.

7) I was very rel__ved when the th__f was caught.

8) Mr Charles was delighted to rec__ve your letter.

9) Sandra is having a four t__red wedding cake.

10) Sandringham House has won the Hockey sh__ld.

11) Your ach__vement is remarkable for a boy of your age.

12) In the old days, the tribal ch__ftain w__lded considerable power.

Two more exercises follow for those who would like additional practice. Remember that the answers are in the back of the book so that you can check your work. Work through Exercise 69 and examine errors (if any) before attempting Exercise 70.

EXERCISE 69

1) fr__ght
2) retr__ve
3) consc__nce
4) chandel__r
5) __ghty
6) fr__ze
7) effic__nt
8) h__ght
9) th__r
10) v__n
11) r__gn
12) y__ld
13) for__gn
14) w__ght
15) n__ther

EXERCISE 70

1) n__ghbour
2) rel__ved
3) b__ge
4) perc__ve
5) h__rloom
6) forf__t
7) effic__nt
8) h__ress
9) ch__f
10) n__gh
11) sh__ld
12) counterf__t
13) ach__ve
14) p__r
15) sl__gh

Extra K

As we discovered earlier in the chapter on suffixes, c and g can sound hard (**c**at, **g**ot) or soft (**c**inema, **g**enuine).

Before **a**, **o**, **u** the two consonants are hard. Before **e**, **i**, **y** the two consonants are soft.

Read these two words aloud: **icing**, **panicking**.

You will notice that **icing** is pronounced with a soft c (it sounds like s) and **panicking** with a k sound. It is the presence of the k between the c and i that has ensured this.

There are **six words** that require the insertion of k before e, i, y in order to keep the c hard:

bivouac	mimic	picnic
frolic	panic	traffic

k before e, i, y

bivouac	bivouacked	bivouacs
	bivouacking	
frolic	frolicked	frolics
	frolicking	frolicsome
mimic	mimicked	mimics
	mimicking	mimicry
panic	panicked	panics
	panicking	panic-monger
	panicky	panic-stricken
picnic	picnicked	picnics
	picknicking	
	picknicker	
traffic	trafficked	traffics
	trafficking	traffic-less
	trafficker	trafficable

EXERCISE 71

Prepared Dictation on Extra K

Eight thankful but frightened <u>picnickers</u> were rescued this afternoon from a famous <u>picnic</u> site in Cumberland. They had the terrifying experience of seeing a heavy vehicle, quite out of control, careering towards them. The driver <u>panicked</u> completely but a resourceful passenger seized the controls and managed to brake at the last moment. It was a miracle that there were no casualties. The liaison between the emergency services was most impressive and rescue vehicles arrived promptly despite heavy Bank Holiday <u>traffic</u>. All concerned were taken to a neighbouring cottage hospital for routine medical checks. 'No more <u>picnics</u> for us!' was the unanimous verdict of the lucky holiday-makers.

Be careful with these!

1) frighten**e**d

2) car**ee**ring

3) pass**e**nger

4) man**a**ged

5) mom**e**nt

6) l**iai**son

7) emerg**e**ncy

8) ar**r**ived

9) conc**e**rned

10) un**a**nimous

Revision words

11) **ei**ght
12) thank**ful**
13) experi**ence**
14) resourc**eful**
15) vehi**cle**
16) comple**te**ly
17) s**ei**zed
18) mira**cle**
19) casual**ties**
20) n**ei**ghbouring

Words often mispronounced

Many quite straightforward words are misspelt because they are not pronounced correctly. Study the following carefully. Do you mispronounce any? If you can correct the way you say the word, your spelling of it will most probably improve.

You could have a spelling quiz when the class feels confident enough to tackle it.

1) ane**m**one
2) ar**c**tic
3) **as**phalt (the first syllable pronounced <u>ass</u> not <u>ash</u>)
4) aspirin (three syllables)
5) athletics (don't put in an extra syllable after <u>ath-</u>)
6) burglar (don't put in an extra syllable after <u>burg-</u>)
7) categ**o**ry (four syllables, think of categ**o**rical)
8) ches**t**nuts
9) cho**c**olates
10) chrysanthe**mum**
11) contempo**r**ary (five syllables)
12) despe**r**ate (three syllables)
13) deteri**or**ate (five syllables)
14) di**ph**theria (first syllable pronounced <u>dif</u> not <u>dip</u>)
15) dis**integ**rate (don't insert r in third syllable, root comes from Latin <u>integer</u> (whole))
16) equipment (no t after second syllable)

17) environment
18) expedition (no r in second syllable. Comes from Latin word for <u>foot</u> like **ped**al and **ped**estrian)
19) extra**ordinary** (don't run second and third syllables together)
20) fla**cc**id (pronounced flaksid)
21) Feb**r**uary
22) gene**a**logical (six syllables)
23) gove**rn**ment
24) grad**u**ally (four syllables)
25) han**d**kerchief
26) heredit**a**ry (five syllables)
27) hund**r**ed (two syllables; don't insert e between them)
28) information
29) inte**r**esting (four syllables)
30) itin**e**rary (five syllables)
31) jewel**lery** or jewel**ry** (not pronounced <u>jewlery</u>)
32) lib**r**ary
33) mete**or**ology (six syllables)
34) mischievous (three syllables; don't insert i before last one)
35) ne**ph**ew (ph pronounced f not v)
36) pac**ked** (as in pac**ked** lunch)
37) pantomi**m**e (no n's)
38) pro**b**ably
39) reco**gn**ise
40) san**d**wich
41) se**c**retary (not pronounced <u>secertary</u>)
42) s**ph**ere
43) s**ph**inx
44) su**r**prise
45) tem**p**erature (four syllables)
46) tempor**a**ry (four syllables)
47) twel**f**th
48) um**br**ella (three syllables; don't insert e in second syllable)
49) veg**e**table (four syllables; think of veg**e**tarian)
50) vet**e**rinary (five syllables!)

Learning strategies

Use your eyes

- Look really carefully at any word you want to learn by heart. Study it. Break the word up into syllables and notice how the word is put together. Recognising a prefix like **psych-** makes it much easier to learn the beginning of the word. Recognising the base word helps as well, particularly when the pronunciation changes, as in **electric**, **electric**ity, **electric**ian. If you know any Latin, make full use of it in recognising common roots, as in e**loqu**ent and soli**loqu**y. if you've studied French and learnt **beau**, then the English word **beau**tiful becomes much easier to spell, and so on. Learn to see patterns and similarities and to use your knowledge of one word to help you with another.

- Concentrate on learning just the part or parts of a word that you *don't* know. If you know the other parts of it and you can remember them easily, you don't need to expend energy on them! There are various strategies to help you remember the difficult bits:

  a) Underline or highlight the tricky part of the word when you write it in your spelling notebook. Your eye will then be drawn to it whenever you turn the page.

  b) You may be able to see words within words and with any luck this will get you over the difficult bit.

piece	(i.e. as in 'a **pie**ce of **pie**')
separate	(it's the fourth letter that people get wrong. Remember it's **a** by saying 'There's **a rat** in sep**a**rate')
Principal	(a̲l̲ as in 'my **pal**, the Princi**pal**')
hear	(not he̲r̲e̲! Remember 'you h**ear** with your **ear**')

104

secretary   (not secertary! Remember 'A
                     secretary can keep a **secret**')

You'll learn to devise others. They are a real help when your mind goes blank!

c) Sometimes it's just one letter that causes the trouble and a daft phrase is all you need to enable you to remember it. I've had trouble myself with remembering how to spell idiosyncrasy. I began to get annoyed at having to look it up *every* time. Was it c or was it s? No mnemonic seemed to help because I could never remember the mnemonic! Then I hit on one that works really well for me and I can remember every time (Silly me! It's idiosyncrasy). Other people's mnemonics won't necessarily work for you and you won't always devise a foolproof one at first attempt, but do persevere.

Another word that causes difficulty with c's and s's is ne**c**es**s**ary. I learnt it by reminding myself that **c** came **1**st (relatively speaking) in the alphabet and **s** came **2**nd but most of my pupils who find the word tricky prefer to remember the phrase '**a** collar and **a pair of** socks'.

d) Try writing several possible ways of spelling a word and see if one 'looks right'. Sometimes this can be the best way and it's marvellous when you can rely on your eye to judge what is correct.

- When you watch television, be aware how often words appear on the screen as well as pictures. Words appear on the weather map, to accompany news items, in commercials, as sub-titles and so on. This visual reinforcement of spelling patterns can be very useful indeed. Allow yourself to be receptive.

- Take an interest in words and their derivations and their idiosyncrasies. Occasionally you'll see short comments like the one overleaf in your local paper.

VIRGING ON THE RIDICULOUS

Many *Express & Echo* readers thought they had spotted a howler in the main front page headline in yesterday's later editions.

The fact is that the post of virger at Exeter Cathedral — and some other cathedrals — is spelt with an i, compared with the more usual verger at other cathedrals and churches.

It is even more confusing at Canterbury, where there is a virgir: not a lot of people know that!

Express & Echo, 15 August 1990

Out-of-the way knowledge like this can give you confidence, and confidence can be very supportive.

● Enjoy the unintentional humour that occasional misprints in newspapers can cause. It's often rather a vulgar humour! Esther Rantzen's *That's Life* on television and Barry Took's *The News Quiz* on Radio 4 have some very funny examples sent them by viewers and listeners. Perhaps you will spot something they can use. Keep an eye on the classified advertisements in your local paper. They're often proof-read rather hastily and mistakes can slip through. *The Guardian* is a national newspaper famous for its misprints!

IN BRIEF

LEARN TO MAKE WORDS YOUR FRIENDS RATHER THAN YOUR ENEMIES.

Use your ears

- You may find you have a strong auditory memory and learn best from hearing things rather than seeing them. Utilise this by chanting words aloud letter by letter and learning them that way. Certainly most people have learnt to spell **Wednesday** by saying the word aloud *as it's spelt*: Wed-**nes**-day. This method can help with other words too for some people.

  Make sure you are pronouncing words correctly on other occasions.

  It's fun distorting words in order to learn them but if you mispronounce words in ignorance and then write what you say, you're doomed to failure. **Mischievous** is very commonly misspelt, as <u>mischievious</u>, as we discovered earlier in this chapter, because people add an extra syllable before –ous. Get your pronunciation sorted out if that's leading you into error.

- Use the pronunciation of companion words to help you out. If, for example, you want to spell **sign**, there's no difficulty in remembering the silent g if you think of the associated words, si**g**nal, si**g**nature and si**g**nificant, when the **g** is pronounced loud and clear. Think of words in families; it helps you to see a pattern, a ground plan, of what can otherwise seem to be a jungle.

- Try to remember spoken words of advice as a memory aid. A student of mine once claimed he could hear my disembodied voice as he struggled with the spelling of **definite** during an exam. He could remember my saying, somewhat mechanically because I often said it (!), 'There is **no** a in <u>definite</u>'. He said it was almost like having me there beside him as a living dictionary. Try recalling spelling advice from friends, teachers, parents etc. when you're having difficulty.

Use your writing hand

- Did you ever learn to spell words when you were very young by tracing them with your finger in a tray of sand? The extra resistance offered by the sand helps to reinforce the feel of writing the letter.

At a later stage, you may even have had to write out three times the correct version of a word you'd misspelt in an essay or exercise. The principle is the same. You're training your hand to cope with the complexities of word formation. It's sometimes worth trusting your hand to 'find the way' if you're hesitating about part of a word.

I've seen some students in the examination room stop and write experimentally *in the air* to check which way their hand wants to write the word.

It is important to make sure you form your letters carefully as you write (remember how deliberately you had to form letters in the sand-tray). If you write sloppily and make one letter hardly different from the next, this reflex hand-brain co-ordination won't work so well.

As a matter of interest, I find that my students' handwriting generally improves as their confidence in spelling increases. Poor spellers often try to disguise their weakness by writing illegibly. I understand why they do it but it's a waste of time.

Always write vividly and interestingly, whether you can spell the words or not. The content of what you write is always what matters most. You are communicating information or emotion or atmosphere or description to the reader and the words you choose will carry the message. If you write illegibly, all this will be lost. Of course, you want your words to communicate accurately by being correctly spelt but spellings can be checked at a later stage.

Proof - reading

When you are happy with the content of your work (you've said what you wanted to say in the way that you wanted to say it), then proof-read it carefully.

You will read through your work initially just to make sure that the content is complete and that the effect is what you intended. The proof-reading stage is when you read through, looking for mechanical errors (spelling, punctuation and grammar). You want to correct all the mistakes you can before writing out your final draft, whether it's a coursework essay or an important letter or report.

Proof-reading is not easy. We tend to read what we *meant* to say and not what is actually there. Part of the trouble is that we read too quickly, we skim through, relying partly on memory. It is very helpful to read your piece *aloud*, if you can. Students who claim to have proof-read their work *will* discover mistakes for themselves if I ask them to read it aloud to me. If you can't read it aloud, read it mentally at that pace.

● Look out for: **missing words**

missing letters, particularly at the ends of words

spelling mistakes

● Use your spelling notebook; use a good dictionary; use an electronic spelling checker; consult teacher, lecturer and friends. If you are in doubt about any word, check it out. If it's a word you are likely to be using again fairly frequently, make sure it's in your spelling notebook with the tricky area highlighted so that you can find it quickly next time.

SPELLING DICTIONARY

If you haven't used a spelling dictionary, then you should look at what's available in a good bookshop. You'll need a conventional dictionary *as well* for all the other things that a dictionary can tell you about a word. The advantage of spelling dictionaries is that they are just for spelling and they anticipate the difficulties spellers are likely to have in *finding* the word as well as spelling the rest of it. It is difficult to find a word in a conventional dictionary if you don't know the first three letters at least. A spelling dictionary accommodates this. If you are looking up **physical** in the fis– section, there'll be a note at the end of that section suggesting you try phys– if you haven't found the word you want. Some spelling dictionaries include misspellings of words in red where you would expect to find them, with the correct version beside it in black. They don't anticipate *all* the possible errors but they get most of them!

Spelling dictionaries can be a very useful aid. Find one that you like and stay with it. It will be a good friend.

ANSWERS

Exercise 1
1) hens   foxes
2) hutches
3) clocks
4) drivers
5) churches   chapels
6) benches
7) houses
8) boxes   fireworks
9) hunches
10) witches   sisters   crones

Exercise 2
1) notices
2) buses   coaches
3) cats   chairs
4) lunches   bonuses
5) tee-shirts   socks
6) pinches   punches   kicks   nudges
7) showers   spells
8) members
9) inches
10) actresses   actors   producers

Exercise 4
1) peloys
2) aromies
3) garulomophities
4) sizergeys
5) bethrays
6) zuys
7) kroskies
8) drahiys
9) carulasophies
10) eszphyxinimities

Exercise 8
1) cargoes   tomatoes   potatoes
2) studios
3) kimonos
4) curios
5) commandos
6) manifestos
7) mottos/mottoes
8) mementos/mementoes
9) gazebos
10) Echoes

Exercise 10
1) wives
2) carafes
3) cliffs
4) halves
5) proofs
6) dwarfs
7) cast-offs
8) flagstaffs
9) knives
10) chiefs

Exercise 11
1) bailiffs
2) lives
3) thieves
4) hoofs/hooves
5) giraffes
6) cafés
7) muffs
8) tariffs
9) sheriffs
10) gulfs

Exercise 12
1) wolves
2) foodstuffs
3) handkerchiefs
4) wharfs/wharves
5) scarfs/scarves
6) roofs
7) shelves
8) reefs
9) thieves
10) calves

Exercise 15
Para 1   before   counties   ways
Para 2   driving
Para 3   reasonable   licence   points
Para 4   aggressive   agreement   suggestion
Para 5   feelings   family   queues   vehicles
Para 6   surely
Para 7   lose   their
Para 8   many
Para 10   sensible
Para 11   policies

Exercise 17
No change

Exercise 18
1) lopped
2) beggar
3) scanning
4) sunny
5) runner

Exercise 19
1) stepped
2) chatting
3) patted
4) stirred
5) glumly
6) muddy
7) rotten
8) droplets
9) fitness
10) witty

Exercise 20
1) sadder/saddest/sadly/sadness
2) thinned/thinner/thinnest/thinning
3) badly/badness
4) hugged/hugging
5) sinful
6) dipped/dipping
7) winsome
8) funny
9) bigger/biggest
10) sunless

Exercise 22
No change

Exercise 23
1) loving
2) participation
3) wavy
4) admirable
5) ignorance

Exercise 24
1) immensely
2) pining
3) useful
4) separately
5) umpiring
6) examination
7) expensive
8) lazy
9) triteness
10) definitely

Exercise 25
1) making
2) improvement
3) breathing
4) aching
5) excitement
6) preparations
7) sharing
8) devotion
9) sincerely
10) nervous

Exercise 26
1) arguing
2) renovation
3) wisely
4) outrageous
5) timing
6) hoping
7) truly
8) ninth
9) dining
10) arrival
11) diver
12) replaceable
13) writing
14) hopeful
15) sincerely

Exercise 27
1) hoping
2) robbing
3) hopping
4) tubing
5) canning
6) biding
7) shinning
8) slopping
9) caning
10) pining
11) sloping
12) planning
13) pinning
14) planing
15) shining

Exercise 28
1) to site
2) to bat
3) to sham
4) to cane
5) to snip
6) to rate
7) to rap
8) to robe
9) to mate
10) to tape

Exercise 31
1) appliance
2) beautiful
3) enjoying
4) healthier
5) creaminess
6) easily
7) variable
8) payment
9) carrier
10) familiar

Exercise 32
1) emptied/emptier/emptying
2) denial
3) alliance
4) studious
5) prayed/prayer/praying
6) penniless
7) fortieth
8) surveyor
9) plentiful
10) destroyed/destroyer/
    destroying

Exercise 34

1) hurrying
2) loveliness
3) readiness
4) mislaid
5) pitied
6) envied
7) copied
8) daily
9) dryness
10) tried
11) parried easily
12) supplied
13) said
14) emptiness

Exercise 38

1) limiting
2) profitable
3) worshipful
4) committal
5) admitting
6) alteration
7) equipping
8) equipment
9) forbidden
10) marketing

Exercise 39

1) beginner
2) allotment
3) forgetting
4) forgetful
5) limitless
6) omitting
7) listening
8) gossiped
9) acquitted
10) regretted

Exercise 40

1) permitted
2) gardening
3) profitable
4) piloted
5) numbered
6) digital
7) outwitted
8) orbited
9) packeted
10) ordered
11) carpeted
12) gossiping
13) submitted
14) transmitted
15) levered
16) petered
17) hammering
18) beginner
19) audited
20) acquitted

Exercise 41

1) cancellation
2) pedalling
3) quarrelsome
4) appalling
5) labelling
6) instalments
7) installments
8) propellant
9) revellers
10) excellent

Exercise 44

Para 1	equally sunny gritty communication different
Para 3	biggest ownership population likelihood
Para 4	firing calculated argument
Para 5	noisier equipped driers
Para 6	housing powerless coming mediation
Para 7	shopping personal
Para 8	unhappily offered
Para 9	isolation surprising

Exercise 47
1) discredit
2) impolite
3) irrelevant
4) ineligible
5) disappear
6) illiterate
7) impious
8) indefinite
9) ignoble
10) irreplaceable
11) illegal
12) irregular
13) informal
14) illegible
15) immature
16) unsophisticated
17) disability/inability
18) immortal
19) irresponsible
20) inactive

Exercise 48
1) prejudices
2) semi-circle
3) overcast
4) overcome
5) displeased
6) aloud
7) avert
8) disappointed
9) aground
10) dishevelled
11) although
12) withhold
13) misspellings
14) overrate/underrate
15) always

Exercise 51
1) effect
2) affect
3) effect
4) effect
5) affect
6) affect
7) effect
8) affect
9) effect
10) effect
11) affect
12) effect
13) affect   affect
14) affect
15) effect
16) effect
17) affect
18) effect
19) affect
20) effect

Exercise 52
1) its
2) it's
3) its
4) It's
5) its
6) its
7) it's
8) It's
9) its
10) It's
11) It's
12) its
13) its
14) Its
15) It's
16) It's
17) It's
18) its
19) Its
20) its

Exercise 53
1) licence
2) licence
3) license
4) licence

115

5) licence
6) licence
7) licence
8) licence
9) license
10) licence

15) past
16) passed
17) passed
18) past
19) passed
20) past

Exercise 54
1) lose
2) loose
3) loose
4) lose
5) loose
6) lose
7) loose
8) lose
9) loose
10) Loose
11) loose
12) loose
13) loose
14) lose
15) lose
16) loose
17) lose
18) lose
19) loose
20) lose

Exercise 56
1) passed
2) past
3) past
4) past
5) passed
6) past
7) past
8) passed
9) passed
10) passed
11) past
12) passed
13) passed
14) past
15) past
16) past
17) past
18) passed
19) past
20) passed

Exercise 55
1) passed
2) past
3) past
4) past
5) past
6) passed
7) past
8) past
9) passed
10) past
11) past
12) Past
13) passed
14) passed

Exercise 57
1) practice
2) practise
3) practise
4) practice
5) practice
6) practice
7) practice
8) practise
9) practice
10) Practise

Exercise 58

1) They're
2) There
3) there
4) they're
5) there
6) they're
7) their
8) they're
9) there
10) there
11) There
12) their
13) there
14) There
15) Their
16) there
17) There
18) their
19) Their
20) they're

Exercise 59

1) They're
2) their
3) their
4) There
5) there
6) Their
7) their
8) there
9) They're
10) There
11) They're
12) their
13) they're
14) There
15) there
16) their
17) They're
18) their
19) there
20) their

Exercise 60

1) to   to
2) too   to
3) to
4) to
5) too
6) two   too
7) to   to
8) to
9) too
10) too   to
11) Too   to
12) Two
13) to   to
14) too
15) Two   to
16) too
17) too
18) To   too
19) to
20) too   to

Exercise 61

1) too
2) too   to
3) to
4) to
5) too
6) to
7) too
8) too   to
9) to
10) to
11) too
12) two
13) too
14) Two
15) to
16) too
17) to
18) to

Exercise 62

1) Where
2) where
3) were
4) were
5) where
6) were
7) Where
8) Were
9) were
10) where
11) where
12) Were
13) where
14) where
15) were
16) were
17) where
18) where
19) Where
20) were

Exercise 63

1) Where
2) where
3) where
4) Were
5) were
6) were   where
7) were
8) Where
9) were   where
10) Were
11) were
12) where   were
13) where
14) where
15) were
16) where
17) Where   were
18) Where
19) were
20) were
21) Were

Exercise 64

1) too
2) past
3) Were
4) their
5) Where
6) to   lose
7) were
8) loose
9) lose
10) It's   too   to   to
11) It's   they're
12) They're
13) It's
14) passed
15) it's   too
16) its
17) Its
18) their
19) passed

Exercise 65

1) clothes
2) of
3) quite
4) to   buy   their
5) knew
6) seem
7) quite   sure
8) Who's
9) You're
10) your
11) know
12) accept

Exercise 66

1) reins
2) eight
3) Cavalier
4) received
5) retriever
6) conceited
7) pierce

8) heir
9) their
10) friend

Exercise 67
1) perceive
2) skein
3) deceit
4) ceiling
5) reindeer
6) field
7) grieve
8) brief
9) conceive
10) veil

Exercise 68
1) niece eighteen
2) priest Sheila
3) piercing shriek audience
4) neighbour believes
5) sovereign reigned
6) Eight reindeer sleigh
7) relieved thief
8) receive
9) tiered
10) shield
11) achievement
12) chieftan wielded

Exercise 69
1) freight
2) retrieve
3) conscience
4) chandelier
5) eighty
6) frieze
7) efficient
8) height
9) their
10) vein
11) reign
12) yield
13) foreign
14) weight
15) neither

Exercise 70
1) neighbour
2) relieved
3) beige
4) perceive
5) heirloom
6) forfeit
7) efficient
8) heiress
9) chief
10) neigh
11) shield
12) counterfeit
13) achieve
14) pier
15) sleigh